Th

From thoughtful personal stories of seemingly intractable problems to a wealth of tools that can help you develop your own solutionary skills, *The Solutionary Way* is filled with both extensive examples of the problems being addressed, along with potential solutions that can be implemented. Read this book. Become a solutionary.

—Shariff Abdullah, author, *Creating a World that Works for All*

In *The Solutionary Way*, Zoe Weil has woven an inspiring and wonderfully usable guide to living a virtuous and productive life in a fast-forward century that seems designed to confuse, paralyze, and divide. I particularly love her focus on progress-making as a practice and mindset, not gauged through a foreseen set of measurable outcomes. A lot of problems are posed when fitting upwards of 9 billion people on a finite planet, but if even a fraction of those humans become humane solutionaries, I see a bright future ahead.

—Andrew Revkin, *New York Times* environmental journalist, and co-author, *The Human Planet: Earth at the Dawn of the Anthropocene*

Some books give us what we want, and some give us what we need. *The Solutionary Way* gives us both: A path toward a more ethical, meaningful life and a process toward a future where everyone, human and nonhuman, can thrive.

—Moby, musician and activist

To address the sentient world's biggest challenges, it's not enough to inspire people. We've got to equip people. That means providing tools to build skills and the motivation to use those skills. Which is exactly what this book does. Practicing the solutionary way will benefit everybody—from you to your loved ones to our more-than-human roommates on this shared Earth.

—Irshad Manji, founder, Moral Courage College, and bestselling author, *Don't Label Me*

As an antidote to the often siloed and quick-fix solutions offered to address the compounding crises plaguing Earth today, in *The Solutionary Way* Zoe Weil invites readers to slow down, step back, and look at the larger interwoven systems we're caught in, and then to devise solutions that elevate the rights and wellbeing of the planet, people, and animals. Zoe offers a multitude of angles from which to diagnose problems so that we can minimize the unintended harmful consequences that may accompany our proposed solutions.

—Nandita Bajaj, M.Ed., executive director, Population Balance

If you are someone who sometimes feels despondent and even despairing about the state of our society and our world, this book is for you. In these times, many of us have felt hope for a peaceful and healthy future becoming increasingly remote. But this book showed me that even with all that is going so wrong in our world, it is far more possible than most of us think to take a life path that is clear, inspiring, practical—and leads us toward a world where all life can thrive.

—John Robbins, president, Food Revolution Network
and author, *Diet For A New America*

Just as hope is a pipe dream without action, an equitable, sustainable future may be a pipe dream without this solutionary blueprint of Zoe Weil's book.

—Robert Shetterly, founder, Americans Who Tell the Truth

I've spent decades working on behalf of people, animals, and the environment, and I've discovered that determining the best strategies is essential to having the biggest impact. This may sound obvious, but it can be challenging to find the most effective approaches that also align with your skillset and concerns. *The Solutionary Way* provides a framework for developing and pursuing solutions that lead to humane and sustainable systems that can endure. I give this book my highest recommendation.

—Bruce Friedrich, co-founder and president, Good Food Institute

Zoe Weil moves us to expand our compassion and challenges us to become what she calls solutionaries who can change the world. Through her words and example, she shares her many hopes and dreams for a more humane future that we can build together.

—Paul Chappell, executive director, Peace Literacy Institute

As a conservationist and documentary filmmaker, I'm always looking for strategic ways to address the grave challenges we face. I believe that if we embrace the solutionary process described in this book we will be on our way to building communities, nations, and a world where people, animals, and nature can thrive. Read this book for yourself and for our global future. Then put it into practice so we can build a healthy world together.

—Susan Rockefeller, artist and
award-winning documentary filmmaker

The Solutionary Way is not just a vision for a more humane world but also offers a positive and practical guide for anyone to become an active contributor to positive change through evidence-based optimism and ethical problem-solving.

—Kiran Bir Sethi, founder, The Riverside School
and Design for Change

THE
SOLUTIONARY
WAY

**Transform Your Life,
Your Community, and
the World for the Better**

ZOE WEIL

Foreword by Dr. Jane Goodall

new society
PUBLISHERS

Cover design by Diane McIntosh.

Cover illustration: © iStock (background #1365741141, dandelion #49021 9610) Chapter title illustration: iStock: 1146828627 © Ksana-gribakina

Printed in Canada. First printing June, 2024.

Inquiries regarding requests to reprint all or part of *The Solutionary Way* should be addressed to New Society Publishers at the address below. To order directly from the publishers, please call 250-247-9737 or order online at https://www. new society.com.

Any other inquiries can be directed by mail to:
New Society Publishers
P.O. Box 189, Gabriola Island, BC V0R 1X0, Canada
(250) 247-9737

LIBRARY AND ARCHIVES CANADA CATALOGUING IN PUBLICATION
Title: The solutionary way : transform your life, your community, and
   the world for the better / Zoe Weil ; foreword by Dr. Jane Goodall.
Names: Weil, Zoe, author. | Goodall, Jane, 1934- writer of foreword.
Description: Includes bibliographical references and index.
Identifiers: Canadiana (print) 20240319524 | Canadiana (ebook)
   20240319532 | ISBN 9780865719989 (softcover) | ISBN
   9781550927917 (PDF) | ISBN 9781771423878 (EPUB)
Subjects: LCSH: Social change. | LCSH: Social action. | LCSH: Social
   advocacy. | LCSH: Problem solving.
Classification: LCC HM831 .W45 2024 | DDC 303.4—dc23

Funded by the Government of Canada   Financé par le gouvernement du Canada | Canadä

New Society Publishers' mission is to publish books that contribute in fundamental ways to building an ecologically sustainable and just society, and to do so with the least possible impact on the environment, in a manner that models this vision.

We are the flood, and we are the ark.

—Jonathan Safran Foer

Contents

Solutionary

Noun

1. A person who identifies inhumane, unjust, and/or unsustainable societal systems and then develops solutions to transform them so that they do the most good and least harm for people, animals, and the environment.

2. A person who brings critical, systems, strategic, and creative thinking to bear in an effort to create positive changes that are equitable, restorative, and humane for all affected.

3. A person who seeks to contribute to humane and sustainable systems by making personal choices that support such systems.

Adjective

1. Pertaining to or characterized by solving problems in a strategic, comprehensive way that does the most good and least harm for all affected.

2. Innovative and far-reaching in a positive way for people, animals, and the environment.

Foreword

Z OE WEIL opens this important book with the sentence "A better world is possible." This belief underlies all my work. I am convinced that we must address the critical issues that this book highlights, such as the need for humane and environmentally responsible production of food, voting rights for all, and alternatives to animal testing for biomedical and other forms of research. There are dire problems facing us in all these areas and many more, but despite the challenges, we must not lose hope. For if we lose hope, we become apathetic and do nothing to promote change. And if young people lose hope, we are doomed. That is why the message in *The Solutionary Way* is so important.

In 1991, I founded the Roots & Shoots humanitarian and environmental youth program in Dar es Salaam, Tanzania, when twelve high school students came to me with concerns about problems in their community. They felt powerless to help. I suggested they bring together their friends who felt the same, and at that meeting Roots & Shoots was born. We decided the main message would be that every individual matters and makes an impact on the planet (for good or bad) every day. And that because all these issues are interconnected, each group would choose three projects—one to help people, one to help animals, and one to help the environment. Or a project encompassing all three. Today that program, with members from kindergarten through university and beyond, is active in some seventy countries. These young people are my greatest reason for hope. Once they understand the problems and are empowered to take action in a program of their choice, they roll up their sleeves and get to work. Everywhere they are making a difference. Their energy, determination, and compassion are inspiring. Hundreds of thousands of young people are Roots & Shoots members, and there are many other youth groups around the world. They are indeed "Solutionaries," identifying problems and developing solutions. I urge you all to join them in building a better world.

During one of my visits to Tanzania, we organized a meeting of different Roots & Shoots groups from around Dar es Salaam so that they could share their projects and encourage and inspire each other. We do this as often as possible in all countries. At the end of that meeting, the young people got together and shouted "Together we can!"—meaning together we can save the world. I told them, "Yes, absolutely we can. But will we?" This startled them, but they understood what I meant. Then I led them in a rousing "Together we can. Together we will!" And now, given how urgently we need change, we've added "Together we must!" As you read this book, keep this rallying cry in your heart. "Together we can! Together we will! Together we must!"

Jane Goodall, PhD, DBE
Founder—the Jane Goodall Institute
& UN Messenger of Peace

Preface:
A Better World Is Possible

A BETTER WORLD IS POSSIBLE. We have the ability to develop sustainable and humane food, production, energy, and other systems. We can end poverty and treat all people equitably. We can learn to solve conflicts without violence and create enduring peace. We can usher in a culture of compassion toward animals, slow the rate of extinction, and restore ecosystems.

How can we build this better world? By becoming solutionaries.

This book makes a bold promise: If you become a solutionary, in addition to making important contributions in your community and world that lead to a healthier, happier future for others, your own life will be enriched. You will have tools for bridge-building and meaning-making. You will make new friends and build collaborative relationships. You will develop a greater sense of agency and efficacy. This is not a feel-good book, but you are likely to feel better if you read it, put it into practice, and share the solutionary process with others.

I wrote this book for people who are already working to create change, as well as those who are frustrated, frightened, and furious but haven't figured out how to channel these emotions into positive actions. I wrote it for those who are despondent and even despairing about the state of their communities, countries, and continents with the pledge that meaningful accomplishments and evidence-based optimism are the likely outcomes as you develop solutions to problems. I wrote it for Gen Z, millennials, Gen X, and baby boomers, because we all have a role to play in building a better future.

If you are someone who already identifies as a changemaker and wants new tools to be more effective and strategic, you'll find these tools in the pages that follow. If you are feeling heartbroken about cruelty, outraged about injustice, and infuriated about environmental destruction, you will find a meaningful path forward. If you're maddened by systems that are inhumane and myopic, you'll discover how to transform these systems. If you are personally experiencing injustice and inequity, you'll learn a process to help solve problems that are directly affecting you, your family, and your community.

Whatever motivated you to pick up this book, I offer you the solutionary way. It will lead you on an important and hope-inducing journey. Along the way, you'll meet others walking beside you. Your destination? A world where all life can thrive.

Introduction:
Bad and Better at the Same Time

I N 2012—before the COVID pandemic, before wildfires were regularly destroying forests and communities in countries across the globe,
before hard-won rights were being rolled back, before polarization had
become so extreme it seemed we could barely come together to solve much
of anything, before childhood anxiety and depression were reaching epi-
demic numbers—I was invited to speak at a middle school in Connecticut.

I asked the fifth and sixth graders to tell me what they thought were
the biggest problems in the world, and I wrote down what they said on
a whiteboard until the board was completely full. Their list was similar
to virtually every other group I'd asked, whether children or adults. One
boy said "sex trafficking," though he had not been learning about this at
school. I asked the children to raise their hands if they thought we could
solve the problems they listed. Of the forty-five children, only five raised
their hands.

This was the most sobering moment in my then almost thirty-year
career as a humane educator—someone who teaches about the interconnected issues of human rights, environmental sustainability, and animal
protection and educates people to be solutionaries. I thought to myself:
If these children can't even imagine us solving the problems they named,
what will motivate them to try to make a difference?

I knew I had to do something to restore their hope, so I asked the students to close their eyes and imagine themselves sitting on a park bench
on a beautiful day at the end of a long and well-lived life. I painted a
picture of the scene: The air and waterways around them were clean. The
birds were singing. Species were recovering from the brink of extinction.
There hadn't been a war in more years than they could remember. No

one went to bed hungry. We had learned to treat each other and other animals with compassion.

Then I asked them to imagine a child coming up to them and joining them on the park bench. I told them that the child had been studying history in school and had been learning about darker times, times they themselves had lived through. The child had all sorts of questions about how things had gotten so much better. Then I asked them to imagine the child asking this final question:

> *"What role did you play in helping to bring about
> this better world?"* [1]

I let them respond to the child in their mind before asking them—with their eyes still closed—to raise their hands if now they could imagine us solving the problems they listed on the whiteboard. This time, forty hands went up in the air. Envisioning a peaceful, healthy world, and knowing that they and the other children in the room would have a role in creating such a future, was enough to restore their hope.

A few years later, I was in Guadalajara, Mexico, to speak at a conference. The day before the conference began, I visited the school that was hosting the event. When I arrived I was invited to talk to some of the fifth graders. Remembering the time I'd spoken to the fifth and sixth graders in Connecticut, I asked these children to raise their hands if they thought we could solve the problems in the world. This time, every hand flew up in the air.

What was different?

Their teacher had been teaching them—in age-appropriate ways—about what was happening on our planet, specifically to our environment, and had been engaging them—also in age-appropriate ways—in solving environmental problems. Their school had installed solar panels, created a composting system for their food waste, and was utilizing large water jugs to refill reusable containers instead of using single-use water bottles. They knew problems could be solved because they had been solving them. They were learning to be solutionaries.

—◊◊◊—

On the day I began writing this book in February 2022, this is what was being reported in the news: Russia was on the brink of invading Ukraine. COVID-19 was killing approximately 2,500 people every day in the United States alone. Canadians opposed to vaccine mandates were blocking the busiest US–Canada border crossing between Windsor, Ontario, and Detroit, Michigan, which in turn was causing factories to shut down. Inflation in the United States was at the highest level in forty years.

Meanwhile, what was barely in the news that day were reports about the planet heating up, with too little being done to stop it, even though the threat of climate change was so apparent and severe that it was already affecting countless species and millions of people, including in wealthy countries with the financial means to pursue solutions. While climate change would appear in the news every time there was a heat wave, wildfire, or other climate-related disaster, it would disappear as soon as the emergency passed.

Nor was it newsworthy that within the year the world's human population would reach eight billion. The month this landmark was reached, there was barely any mention of it at all, even though our population had doubled in fewer than fifty years, creating significant impacts on the ecosystems that support all of us, human and nonhuman.

While there were some reports the day I began this book about human rights abuses, the persistence of slavery perpetrated on tens of millions of people across the globe and the reality that around two billion people lived without access to safely managed drinking water,[2] about 1.6 billion didn't have adequate shelter,[3] and approximately eight hundred million didn't have enough food to eat[4] was largely absent in the media. Perhaps this wasn't newsworthy because it was the norm.

Nor were there news reports about the more than three billion animals killed that day, and every day,[5] around the world, primarily for food, nor about the mercilessness with which they were treated before they had their throats slit or were netted, hooked, suffocated, electrocuted, or boiled alive. The sheer numbers and levels of suffering stagger the imagination, but again, norms aren't news.

As I listened to the report that day about Russia's potential military invasion of Ukraine—which would soon turn into a relentless, bloody conflict—I turned to my husband and said, "I can't believe we still resort to war when we disagree." I may have sounded naive, but I meant it. Even though violent conflicts were occurring all over the world; even though in the country where I live—the United States—there were more guns than people, and in the coming months there would be many mass shootings; even though the US defense budget eclipsed spending on all but social security and healthcare, I found it hard to believe that we still resort to violence and that Russia's president was about to unleash a brutal, immoral invasion of his neighboring country.

Do you see it? Do you feel it? The tragic senselessness of killing each other, other animals, and harming our one and only astonishingly beautiful home?

What's so perplexing is that we have the means to solve our conflicts without violence; to feed all of humanity without cruelty to animals, the oppression of people, or the destruction of the environment; and to live harmoniously on our wondrous planet. Moreover, it does not require anything special to participate in solving our problems. We don't need to be geniuses or saints. We don't need specialized knowledge or an advanced degree. We don't need to be a member of a specific religion or a nonbeliever. There are no citizenship requirements. We don't even need to be especially kind and compassionate or have extra helpings of courage and perseverance (although these don't hurt).

Despite the conflict, suffering, and destruction in our world, the truth is that so much is getting better. I am writing these words as a woman in her sixties. In my own lifetime, I've witnessed enormous positive changes. When I was a child:

- More than half of the people in the world lived in extreme poverty. Today approximately 10% do.
- Less than half of people across the globe had access to electricity.[6] Today more than 90% do.[7]
- In the United States, discrimination based on race was legal. In many states, people of different races could not get married.

But then, when I was three years old, the Civil Rights Act was passed, which ended legal segregation in public places and banned employment discrimination on the basis of race, color, religion, sex, or national origin. Three years later, in its *Loving v. Virginia* decision, the Supreme Court declared that laws banning interracial marriage were unconstitutional.

- Smog and soot covered many American cities, but then the 1970 Clean Air Act was passed reducing particulates, sulfur dioxide, lead, and nitrogen oxides.[8] Air pollutants have since fallen more than 90% in some parts of the country, and improvements in air quality have prevented hundreds of thousands of premature deaths and hospitalizations.[9]

- Fires were breaking out on US rivers and lakes because the water was so polluted, and there was no federal law to stop sewage and industrial chemicals from being dumped into our waterways.[10] But then, in 1972, the Clean Water Act was passed, and waterways in the US are now cleaner than when I was a child.

- Women were only just beginning to aspire to have careers beyond teaching, secretarial work, and nursing. Now, more girls in the US attend college than boys, and around the globe—even in countries where women are still treated as second-class citizens—the vast majority of girls go to school.

- Gay, lesbian, and trans people were mostly closeted. Today, there is marriage equality in the US and in many other countries, and despite current trends to roll back trans rights, many of those rights are codified into laws.[11]

- A relatively small percentage cared about the plight of animals. Now, according to a Gallup poll,[12] most people in the United States believe animals should be protected from abuse.

I don't want to pretend that these positive changes paint a rosy picture. More than seven hundred million people still live in extreme poverty, and nearly 47% of the world's population lives on less than

$6.85 per day.[13] While the Civil Rights Act and Supreme Court decision declaring anti-miscegenation laws unconstitutional were profoundly important steps toward racial justice, structural racism in housing, education, healthcare, incarceration, and other systems persists. Not all US waterways are cleaner. Water pollution, especially from agricultural run-off, is still despoiling waterways and creating dead zones in the ocean, and while the US addressed smog and soot through the Clean Air Act, many other countries have not enacted similar regulations, and the air in their large cities has become terribly polluted through industrialization and congestion. Moreover, the rise in wildfires is periodically creating extreme air pollution. And because of the growing global demand for meat, the number of animals treated cruelly is still increasing, despite the fact that more people support an end to animal abuse.

Nonetheless, the positive changes that have occurred in my lifetime are why, even during a decade in which we have faced a global pandemic; increasing impacts from climate change; growing polarization and conspiracy theories fed by disinformation and misinformation; a rise in hate crimes;[14] rampant inequities; persistent animal abuse; the specter of artificial intelligence going awry; brutal wars and the continued threat of nuclear weapons, I am still stubbornly optimistic.[15]

Advocates for a more equitable, sustainable, peaceful, and humane world are quick to talk about how much injustice and harm continues across the globe. We want everyone to become motivated to make a difference and not to become complacent. If people were to believe that things are better than they appear, then perhaps they might lose their sense of outrage and urgency. Or they might think it's inevitable that things will progress without their personal involvement. They might think, as Dr. Martin Luther King Jr. repeated on more than one occasion, "The arc of the moral universe is long, but it bends toward justice,"[16] and if it is bending toward justice, perhaps they can effortlessly slide down that beautiful arc into a peaceful, equitable, and healthy future without having to involve themselves in the process.

But there is no need to create either/ors. The world can be bad and better at the same time. Injustices, cruelties, violence, and oppressions can still occur even as much is improving. Because I spend my days working for a regenerative planet and a humane future for both people and animals, I'm acutely aware of how far we have to go. Still, I am buoyed by the positive changes that have happened since I was born. They remind me that we can and do make progress, even if progress often feels like two steps forward and one step back.

It's so important to notice the positive changes in our world and elevate those stories where collaboration and cooperation have led to sustainable and humane systems. Despite the advances in social justice, environmental awareness, and animal protection, too many people feel overwhelmed by a sense of doom, and too many of these people are the children, teenagers, and young adults who hold the keys to our collective future. It's essential that young and old alike understand that there is still much that is bad—indeed very, very bad—yet there is much that is better—indeed, astoundingly better! What is better can serve as a reminder to temper pessimism and provide inspiration for the solutionary work that we need to do going forward. To solve the challenges we face; to build truly peaceful societies; to create humane, sustainable, and equitable systems that endure, we need to hitch our good intentions to good thinking and learn how to be solutionaries, which requires a mindset, a value-system, and a practice, all of which can be learned and cultivated.

The Solutionary Way will get you started. It will explain what it means to be a solutionary and how being a solutionary represents next-level change. It will explore the ethical principle of doing the most good and least harm, which is embedded in the solutionary process. It will elucidate the solutionary mindset and lens, the elements of solutionary thinking, the solutionary process itself, and where solutionary ideas are arising and taking hold.

Some readers of this book will be able to adopt "solutionary" as a primary identity that is fully integrated into their profession, community engagement, and personal life. Others may not see a clear path to being a full-time solutionary within their career or workplace but may discover myriad opportunities to bring solutionary thinking and action to their lives, the issues they care about, and to groups with whom they engage regularly.

Each of us is situated within different communities and spheres of influence. These are places where a solutionary community and solutions to persistent problems can emerge. You may be:

- involved with a nonprofit or government agency that could become more strategic in achieving its mission through a solutionary mindset;
- a businessperson or entrepreneur who can bring solutionary thinking to your industry or company;
- working in the media where you have the power to spread solutionary ideas and confront the persistence of either/or framing;
- in healthcare where solutionary approaches are needed to pursue prevention, lower costs, and greater access;
- working in law where pursuing new precedents can create far-reaching change;
- in politics where a solutionary lens can reduce partisanship and advance ideas that will help pave the way for a more democratic and healthy society;
- an educator whose reach is among the most powerful and influential of all professions should you bring the solutionary process to those you teach;
- a visual artist, writer, filmmaker, podcaster, poet, cartoonist, comedian, choreographer, or songwriter who can provoke thinking and inspire action through your art;
- an architect, scientist, engineer, farmer, coder, or working in any number of professions that enable you to transform a system so that it does more good and less harm;
- a member of a religious congregation, service club, 12-step program, fitness regime, and/or community of people who share a hobby where you can find partners on your solutionary journey to address issues that relate to the interests you have in common;
- a student eager to find your solutionary path and collaborate with your fellow learners.

Whoever you are and whatever your work, you can be a solutionary.

Becoming a solutionary isn't rocket science, but it's not easy either. There are many obstacles. Our biology and psychology lead us to resist long-term, systemic, us-*and*-them (rather than us-*versus*-them) thinking, as well as to be able to challenge our cognitive biases and maintain an open and critically thinking mind when faced with differing perspectives. Our globalized economies make solving problems without creating unintended negative consequences challenging. Inequitable, unsustainable, and inhumane systems (from which we are unable to personally extricate ourselves) are interconnected behemoths that make systemic change difficult and often laborious. Nonetheless, we can overcome these obstacles. This book will show you how.

What kind of world do you want to live in? What future do you want to bequeath to the generations of humans and nonhuman animals who will follow us? In your desired world, is there greater peace and equity among people? Does everyone have a home, clean water, and enough nutritious, humanely and sustainably produced food? What's become of the rainforests, the remaining old-growth forests, and the boreal forests? Are oceans becoming cleaner? Do coral reefs still exist? Are marine species recovering? How do we treat sentient animals?

Close your eyes and try to envision this world that you yearn for. And then take heart: there is a way to help build this world. It's the solutionary way.

Chapter 1:

A SOLUTIONARY MINDSET FOR NEXT-LEVEL CHANGE

What I've Learned from Improv Comedy

THE PRIMARY DISPOSITIONS that I believe are essential in the effort to become a solutionary come from what I've learned from improvisational comedy. I'm a huge fan of this art form, not only because I often find it hilarious, but also because it offers meaningful life lessons along with wise approaches to budding solutionaries. This realization came to me when I began taking improv comedy classes with my husband.

There are some basic rules to improv comedy that include the following:

- Build relationships.
- Embrace "Yes, and…"
- Bring the love.
- Help others shine.

With the most minor of suggestions from the audience, such as a location or a made-up title, improvisational actors begin a scene. The first thing these actors will do is establish a relationship. A middle-aged female actor might turn to her young male scene partner and exclaim, "Mom, I've entered us into the parent-child acrobatic competition at school!"

It doesn't matter that the actor does not look like a child or an acrobat or that the mother is male and decades younger. What matters is that a relationship has been established. If the actors are committed to the relationship, the audience will be too.

Perhaps the scene partner says, "Fabulous Brian! We can finally wear the matching pink polka-dot leotards I purchased on ebay!" Now we know that the child is named Brian, Mom may have some binge-shopping habits, and we may have some gender-bending opportunities at hand. The scene is moving forward because the second actor agreed to the premise and added to it.

Brian can resist wearing the pink polka-dotted leotard if she wants, as long as she doesn't deny that these leotards exist and that Mom is excited. Brian might embrace the costume or use Mom's strange shopping choices as a jumping-off point to move the scene along. What Brian won't do if she is a good improv comedian is start an argument. This is because arguments aren't generally that much fun to watch. In improv comedy, love trumps hate, and improvisational comedians usually look for ways to bring the love and help their scene partners shine.

What do these improv comedy rules have to do with cultivating a solutionary mindset? So much!

Build relationships

In order to successfully solve problems with all stakeholders in mind and strive to do the most good and least harm for everyone, we need to be able to communicate effectively and compassionately with one another. In our polarized societies full of either/or and us-versus-them thinking, we routinely clash, turn others into opponents, defend our positions, stop listening, and wind up *preventing* solutionary ideas and action from occurring.

The first step in breaking free of these dysfunctional patterns of behavior is to build relationships with a diverse array of people, and to build these relationships, we must choose to reach outside of our bubbles. Doing so isn't easy and takes practice, and many (if not most) of us generally take the path of least resistance and actively avoid interacting with others whom we consider "them."[17]

To be clear, many people have legitimate and wise reasons to avoid reaching out to people who do not share their views. Power, class, religious, ethnic, gender, and racial dynamics can put those with less power, and who may be frequent victims of bigotry and hate, at risk of harm or retaliation for speaking honestly. This is all the more reason for those who are not at risk of retribution to step up to the challenge of reaching beyond their bubbles so that they can be better advocates and solutionaries. And for those with privileges, whether based on wealth, ability, nationality, race, gender, sexual orientation, et cetera, it's important to recognize the power dynamics that may exist when reaching out to people who are relatively less privileged and to consider how to listen more and cede power in order to create a welcoming space for meaningful connection and collaboration.

In 2016, shortly after the election in which Donald Trump won the electoral college vote and became the president of the United States, I was giving a keynote presentation at a conference in Boston. One of the other keynote speakers was a well-known Harvard professor. During his presentation, he mentioned that he didn't know anyone who had voted for Trump. Because he lived in the liberal bastion of Cambridge, Massachusetts, worked as a professor in a progressive department, and was surrounded by like-minded people, I shouldn't have been surprised, but I was. I also felt disappointed. Was he subtly suggesting that Trump supporters were not worth knowing?

He wasn't alone. During the campaign, Hillary Clinton said during a speech to supporters: "to just be grossly generalistic, you could put half of Trump's supporters into what I call the basket of deplorables. Right? … The racist, sexist, homophobic, xenophobic, Islamophobic you name it…."[18]

We know what happened. That statement may have led her to lose the election (though not the popular vote), and some Trump supporters proudly display the name "deplorables" on bumper stickers and T-shirts to this day. The divisiveness in the United States grew.

While I did not vote for Donald Trump, I knew plenty of people who had. Some were new friends of mine from the CrossFit affiliate I'd joined that year, and they were not deplorable. Among them were some of the most generous and welcoming people I knew. The summer before the election, when a friend left our CrossFit gym because there were Trump supporters among us, I was dismayed. She was shutting the door on conversation and understanding and doubling down on living inside her bubble. Had she been a member of a marginalized community, subject to the increased bigotry that arose during the campaign and its aftermath, and at risk for hostility at our gym, I would have felt differently, but that was not the case.

Meanwhile, I felt like I'd never had such a powerful opportunity to practice being a solutionary. I welcomed the chance to build deeper relationships with people who had different views from my own and to be the humane educator I claimed to be. One of my new friends from CrossFit—who voted for Trump in 2016 (though not in 2020)—went on to become one of my closest friends and a generous supporter of my work. Our regular conversations led to both of us learning, growing, thinking more carefully and deeply, and striving to come up with more solutionary ideas than what were being fed to us by polarizing media.

Politics is just one arena where building relationships across differences is helpful in becoming a solutionary. There are all sorts of values and beliefs that lead us to separate ourselves in order to spend all or most of our time with our in-groups and consume the media preferred by those groups.

Having dedicated my life to advancing social justice, animal protection, environmental sustainability, and women's rights, I have been part of a lot of in-groups. It has taken a great deal of commitment to the value of building relationships for me to seek out friendships with people who kill or harm animals recreationally, who fight against a woman's ability to have an abortion, who oppose environmental efforts and regulations, and who say things that I consider to be bigoted. But I know that unless I build such relationships, I will be more likely not only to stereotype, caricature, and possibly even vilify others who have different beliefs but also to miss the opportunities to expand my own awareness and understanding as well as to influence people in positive ways.

To avoid stereotyping, caricaturing, and vilifying others, I remind myself of a few things:

- I don't want to be stereotyped, caricatured, and vilified myself.
- I'm not a paragon of virtue and have plenty of arenas where I can and should do better.
- The great majority of people share a commitment to such virtues as compassion, generosity, courage, perseverance, integrity, and kindness, even if we differ on how they can best be put into practice.

- When I "other" someone, I close the door on building the bridges that may lead to solutionary thinking and action.

If you are reading this book, there's a good chance that you have strong opinions about various issues and are active in some way to make a difference by advancing your beliefs and advocating for the issues that concern you. Building relationships will help you succeed.

Embrace "Yes, and..."

"Yes, and..." refers to the practice of "agreeing" with one's scene partner in an improvisational sketch and adding to the prompts they offer. In the example I used to illustrate an improv scene, the actor who was called "Mom" immediately became Mom. In other words, he implicitly said "yes" to the role of Mom. Then he implicitly said "and" by adding to the scene with new ideas. In improv comedy, experienced actors avoid saying "but" or denying the prompts they are given by their scene partners. If they were to deny their scene partner's ideas, the scene wouldn't go anywhere, and the audience wouldn't enjoy watching it.

What does this have to do with being a solutionary? If we are to successfully and effectively address and solve problems with the fewest unintended negative consequences, we need to consider the perspectives of all stakeholders. Given the human tendency to pit "us" against "them" and to argue and debate with (and too often belittle and disparage) our perceived enemies, there is much to be learned from "yes, and...." When we bring a "yes, and..." disposition, we are actively seeking to understand and agree with whatever we can. In other words, we look for what we are able to say "yes" to and then add what we have to offer by saying "and...".

"Yes, and..." can literally become the language you use in conversations. In discussions with my friend and colleague Mary Pat Champeau, we use this language regularly. We even laugh about it because when one of us says "yes, and..." we know this means we have points of divergence. We also know that we are listening to, acknowledging, and recognizing the value of what the other person has just said, and it's our responsibility to add nuance, ideas, and other ways of thinking, not to reject the other person's thoughts if we disagree. The language itself primes us to think ever more critically, systemically, strategically, and wisely.

Mary Pat and I agree on most issues, so embracing "yes, and..." isn't usually challenging for us, but I have many friends with whom I disagree strongly about highly charged issues. For example, as alluded to previously, I'm pro-choice, and I have friends who are pro-life. Yet, even with such a divisive issue, it's possible to bring a "yes, and..." approach. Virtually everyone can agree that it would be best if there were as few girls and women as possible facing an unwanted pregnancy. In this sense, it should be easy for pro-choice advocates like me to say "yes" to someone who doesn't want fetuses aborted. Then I can add the "and..." to consider how we can significantly reduce the number of girls and women becoming pregnant who do not wish to have a child. Meanwhile, pro-life advocates concerned about the ability of fetuses to suffer during abortion can potentially be persuaded to support Plan B—the morning-after pill—which can end an early pregnancy during the embryonic stage before there is a fetus that could potentially experience pain.

I suspect many are rolling their eyes at this Pollyanna-ish belief that we might find any common ground on this issue, but solutionaries who are pro-choice and those who are pro-life may want to give it a try. I have successfully influenced pro-life advocates to support Plan B by listening to their concerns about abortion, showing respect, and working to find a place of agreement. While this "yes, and..." example doesn't address the religious belief, which many pro-life people hold, that a fertilized egg is a human being deserving of the full protection of law, it still represents a step toward finding *some* common ground ("yes") and seeking nuance in responding in a solutionary way amidst conflicting beliefs and values ("and"). By bringing a "yes, and..." disposition both to interactions with others, as well as when addressing persistent problems, many of the obstacles to solutionary thinking and action are removed, and new avenues toward solutions begin to appear.

Bring the love

Conflicts on stage aren't generally funny. Sure, brilliant improvisational comedians like Larry David can pull off arguments with humor (which is pretty much the premise of his show *Curb Your Enthusiasm*), but it's generally funnier to watch love rather than hate unfold. That's why improv comedians make every effort to bring the love.

How does this translate into a solutionary mindset? For many, if not most of us, it is easier to focus on the negative, such as ill-feelings, frustrations, and resentments, than on the positive. How quickly we judge others and feel anger. Litter on the ground? Only a jerk would leave their trash for others to deal with. Cut off in traffic? What a contemptible person. They voted for that dolt? Idiot.

And then there's the Internet, where distance allows us to enter our psychic underworld and unleash our worst qualities through the comfort of our keyboards as we make short-tempered, sarcastic, and mean-spirited comments (or much worse) online. We may think we're not really being nasty or offensive as we criticize, but are we bringing the love?

This is the hardest improv rule to adopt as a solutionary because anger about the problems we're trying to address is often sudden and overwhelming. Yet we have a choice about whether to indulge our worst qualities or to embrace our best.

After Vladimir Putin ordered the invasion of Ukraine, and I was constantly consuming news about the atrocities perpetrated on Ukrainians by the Russian army, my husband and I heard a group of people speaking Russian (a language I love, and which I've studied) in the parking area by a trail in Acadia National Park near where we live. I was blindsided by a pounding heart and a sudden feeling of anger. My mind immediately jumped to judgmental questions: Did they support Putin's invasion? What were they doing to help Ukrainians? Why were they going on a leisurely walk in Acadia instead of risking their comfort to end the brutality of their president? And how was it that I—a person who adores a young man in Russia whom my family tried to adopt for many years when he was a boy—could suddenly be Russophobic?

While all these thoughts, feelings, and questions were swirling through my racing brain, one of the men approached me to ask a question about the hike we'd just been on. I stuffed down my anger and reminded myself that I knew nothing about these people. I didn't even know if they were Russian, since not all Russian speakers are. They could have been Ukrainians!

Mentally noting my own hypocrisy, I also realized that I had not asked myself what I was doing to help Ukraine at that moment, having just gone on my own leisurely walk. As friendly as I could be, I advised these Russian-speaking visitors about the trail. I brought the love. I could have indulged my anger and assumptions and snubbed them, but who would that have served? Not me. Not these strangers. Not Ukrainians. No one. "Bringing the love" didn't just serve the people who asked my advice; it did me a world of good, too.

Help others shine

The best improvisers focus on helping their scene partners shine. They look for ways not to showcase themselves but rather to create scenes that build on the gems their partners share. When everyone is doing this, everyone wins.

The more we shine light on and share goodness, the more we cause it to grow and spread. I can feel the cynics rolling their eyes at such trite "wisdom," but there is a deep truth embedded in this improv comedy rule. To actively seek to shine light on those doing good is to reframe the way we see the world and interact within it and to set the stage for promulgating more good. So look for those doing good in communities, regions, and nations and observe, learn from, emulate, and amplify their voices and actions.

Cultivating a Solutionary Mindset

In 2009, I was listening to the radio when I heard an announcement for an upcoming "Oxford-style debate" sponsored by the Open to Debate (formerly Intelligence Squared) series and held at New York University. The topic of the debate was this statement: "America is to blame for Mexico's drug war." There would be experts representing two sides: the side that agreed with the statement and the side that disagreed.

I marveled at the time and effort that would go into this debate, all while the drug war raged in Mexico, and while so many people were dying through drug-related violence (not to mention through drug use). The idea that Mexico's drug war would be reduced to an either/or question and that a good use of brilliant minds and the public's time would be to participate in such a debate rather than work together to try to solve the problem of the drug war seemed misdirected to me.

When my son entered high school, one of the requirements for graduation was to participate in a school debate. Students were assigned one side or the other of a fabricated either/or scenario and told to research and strive to "win." I asked myself, toward what end?

While I recognize that people gain useful skills through the debate process, including investigative, critical thinking, communication, analytic, and persuasion skills, they can gain these same skills by working to find solutions to the problems that underlie the debate topic. If instead of only participating in debate, they also collaborated to *solve* those underlying problems, in addition to the skills above, they would also gain skills in systems thinking, strategic thinking, creative thinking, collaboration, cooperation, consensus-building, listening, and of course problem-solving. Rather than a win-lose scenario, they would be striving for a solution in which everyone wins.

Below are other debate topics from the Open to Debate series:

Don't blame teachers' unions for our failing schools

Universal health coverage should be the federal government's responsibility

Clean energy can drive America's economic recovery

Major reductions in carbon emissions are not worth the money

Don't give us your tired, your poor, your huddled masses

Buy American/hire American policies will backfire

Guns reduce crime

Aid to Africa is doing more harm than good

Global warming is not a crisis

Airports should use racial and religious profiling

We should legalize the market for human organs

Anti-Zionism is anti-Semitism

For each statement, the series had experts debate one side or the other, with the audience voting to determine the winner of the debate. Please read through the debate topics above once more, then choose one and ask yourself these questions:

- Why did I choose this topic?
- What is(are) the underlying problem(s) that the debate statement addresses?
- Does the statement adequately identify the actual problem(s)?
- If there are interwoven problems, is it useful to separate out one issue and respond to it in isolation?

Then ask yourself what solutions already exist, whether enacted on a small or large scale anywhere in the world, that have successfully addressed these underlying problems or similar problems. If you don't know, how could you find out? And if solutions exist, consider what knowledge and skills you would need to further implement or extend them. How might these solutions improve your own life and the lives of others?

In essence, this manner of questioning and thinking exemplifies the solutionary mindset. It is a mindset that resists arbitrary either/or statements and seeks to carefully identify underlying problems and approach them as solvable. It is a mindset that is dedicated to careful and thorough research and investigation, and which strives to find strategic solutions that can be implemented on a large scale and spread.

Adoption of such a mindset might seem obvious. Who wouldn't want to approach problems this way? Unfortunately, the solutionary mindset is not our default. To the contrary, either/or side-taking is more often the norm, and as soon as we frame a problem as an either/or, we tend to miss the entire spectrum of possible solutions that exist between and beyond the two sides. Once we have created a binary mindset that reinforces an us-versus-them mentality, we tend to lose a "we" perspective. Binary thinking can also lead people to believe that one side of the debate is "good," and the other side is "bad," with little room for considering a variety of options. Such thinking often becomes a reinforcing feedback loop as we seek to continually bolster our "side," which then further discourages us from collaborating across divides to solve problems.

Either/or thinking is so embedded in US culture that it shows up in most of our systems, especially in our political, media, economic, legal, criminal justice, and even our education system. In the US we have only two viable political parties since the other parties are so small and under-funded that they almost never win national elections and rarely win local elections. Yet it's silly to think there are just two ways of thinking about every issue or problem, and that people will fit neatly into a red or blue basket. Most of us know this, which may be part of the reason why the group of people identifying as Independents continues to grow,[19] but the stranglehold that the two parties have on US politics has led to profound dysfunction in governance and the legislative process.

This means that complex problems with competing interests turn into fierce fights that lead to winners and losers. I often point to an example of this from the 1990s—not because I can't find plenty of more recent examples, but because this example has played out in complex ways that continue to this day (and because it's good to remember that polarization is not a new phenomenon). The conflict I'm referring to was generated by placing the Northern Spotted Owl on the list of threatened species.

In the 1980s, scientists began to notice a severe decline in the popu-lation of the Northern Spotted Owl, and in 1990, the owl was federally listed as threatened under the US Endangered Species Act. This trig-gered the protection of the owls' habitat on federal lands in 1991, which meant that the old growth forests where the owls nest could no longer be logged. Thus began the side-taking. Lawn signs and bumper stickers popped up in the Pacific Northwest with people identifying their alle-giance to *either* the owls *or* the loggers.

It should come as no surprise that the language used was often dis-missive of the concerns of the "other side." Sometimes it was vicious. Politicians joined the fray, and the media amplified the conflict, always pit-ting loggers and owls against one another. It was rare to hear about people coming together to focus on solutions to the job crisis while simultane-ously supporting forest protection. And yet, such a solutionary approach could have worked for the benefit of the great majority of stakeholders.

As one example of such an approach, Amazon conservationist Paul Rosolie, the director of the nonprofit Junglekeepers, was (and continues to be) horrified and heartbroken by the destruction of the Amazon rain-forest from the logging, mining, and agricultural industries. But instead of considering the Indigenous workers employed by those companies as his enemies, he recognized that they had few job options and were doing what they needed to do to support their families. It's not as if they wanted to destroy their rainforest homes. Reaching out to them with respect, empathy, and as potential friends and colleagues, he offered alter-native employment—with significantly higher salaries—as forest rangers rather than forest destroyers. Such collaboration and coalition building to meet mutual goals and needs has served the interests of both Indigenous Amazonians and ensured the protection of an ever-growing swath of Amazon rainforest.[20]

What ended up happening in the Pacific Northwest in the fight be-tween owls and loggers? The old-growth forests were protected—which helped countless species—and thousands of people did indeed lose their jobs, although less than one quarter of what the industry claimed would result.[21] Unfortunately, the Northern Spotted Owl population has con-tinued to decline significantly. This may be due in large part to their previously depleted habitat, but it's also being caused by a competing species—the Barred Owl—which has moved into the Spotted Owl's ter-ritory.[22] Although no longer in the national news, the current either/or debate revolves around whether to kill the Barred Owls, which is what the US Fish and Wildlife Service wants to do. Where once the either/or debate revolved around people versus a species, now it revolves around one owl species versus individual animals of a related owl species.

If you were someone on the "side" of the Northern Spotted Owl during the years in which the conflict was in the news, where are you now? Are you still on the "side" of the Northern Spotted Owl as a species, or does it seem wrong to you to kill individual Barred Owls simply because they are out-competing their cousins? What would it mean to bring a solutionary mindset to these conflicting interests and resist side-taking in favor of finding solutions that do the most good and least harm for all involved?

Having a solutionary mindset doesn't mean that one never takes sides (nor that it will always be possible to find solutions that are good for everyone). That would be an example of yet another either/or. We do not have to choose to be *either* a solutionary *or* a side-t£ survivor Elie Wiesel once said, "We must always take si᷄ helps the oppressor, never the victim. Silence encourages t never the tormented."[23] There are times to take sides anc there are no truly "solutionary solutions"—that is, solutions ᴛnat address the root and/or systemic causes of problems and solve them in ways that have few unintended negative consequences to people, animals, or the environment. But the fact that there aren't always solutions that are truly solutionary doesn't mean there aren't some strategies that are better than others when considering what will do the most good and least harm.

There is another quote that may temper the penchant for absolutist statements in this regard, and it comes from physicist Niels Bohr, who said: "The opposite of a correct statement is a false statement. But the opposite of a profound truth may well be another profound truth."[24]

A solutionary mindset essentially means that, without absolutism, one brings a solutions-focused disposition and attitude to problems and resists being drawn into binary thinking and side-taking—unless, of course, taking a side is the most solutionary answer to a problem. It also means that one brings a solutionary *lens* to problems.

What Is a Solutionary Lens?

At the Institute for Humane Education (IHE), the organization I co-founded and where I work, we describe a solutionary lens as the effort and ability to:

- *see* unsustainable, inhumane, and inequitable systems that are causing problems;
- *recognize* that problems don't exist in isolation;
- *seek* the perspectives of all stakeholders; and
- *focus* on solutions that do the most good and least harm for the people, animals, and ecosystems that are impacted.

So far, I've given an example of an either/or statement (America is to blame for Mexico's drug war) and an either/or conflict between environmentalists and loggers (owls versus jobs). Often, either/ors revolve around concepts and labels that lead to us-versus-them thinking, such as conservative vs. liberal, capitalist vs. socialist, believer vs. atheist, et cetera. Intellectually, we know that there are vastly more nuances embedded in these labels and categories, but emotionally we are often inclined to identify with labels. Yet labels shift and morph over time. If we can recognize that these categories aren't static, it's possible to soften our attachments to them. As the co-founder of the Institute for Humane Education, Rae Sikora, once said: "Wherever you draw the line between us and them, draw it in pencil since you'll likely need an eraser."

The more we create sides to which we can pledge our allegiance, the harder it becomes to bring a solutionary lens to the underlying issues and questions that led to the development of those sides. For example, consider the economic localization movement which advocates "buying local" as the answer to myriad problems.

Author Helena Norberg-Hodge begins her TEDx talk, The Economics of Happiness,[25] with this impassioned plea: "For all of us around the world, the highest priority, the most urgent issue is fundamental change to the economy." She goes on to say, "The change that we need to make is shifting away from globalizing to localizing economic activity."

There are many ways in which localizing economies leads to positive outcomes, and it is enormously valuable to embrace efforts to build healthy and resilient local communities. Yet there's a danger when we believe we've found *the* answer, because we may stop looking through a solutionary lens and become attached to a particular perspective, ideology, or solution.

To illustrate what I mean by this, imagine yourself taking Helena Norberg-Hodge's perspective to heart and believing that our highest priority should be a shift toward localization. Perhaps you'll support farmers' markets and eschew products and foods that have traveled far from where they were produced or grown. You may have heard of the *100-Mile Diet,* a bestselling book by authors Alisa Smith and J.B. MacKinnon, who spent a year eating foods produced within 100 miles of where they lived. You may even subscribe to this diet, even though 100 miles is an arbitrary, if nice round number (that doesn't sound quite as compelling when converted to 161 kilometers). But is such a local diet—and localization beyond food choices—the most solutionary approach to our problems?

While farmers' markets and local food initiatives have certainly been beneficial to farmers, communities, and consumers alike, is it realistic, desirable, or even responsible to advocate localization as the primary path to a healthy, happy economy in general? A full commitment to local foods would mean that in Maine, where I live, people would need to give up coffee, citrus, rice, and so much more, and rely on potatoes, wheat, beans, foraged food, hunted, trapped, netted, and hooked animals, and canned and dried food stored from our relatively brief summers. If we went further and included clothing, such a commitment to localization would mean forgoing cotton and wearing primarily linen clothing and animal hides.

Just as there are important benefits from localization, there are also important benefits from globalization. Medicines developed and produced by scientists working in laboratories in one part of the world are regularly exported to places far away where they are most needed, and the key ingredients in those medicines are often discovered in other parts of the world, such as tropical rainforests.

If localization became our primary focus, what would happen to the Ethiopian coffee farmers depicted in the film *Black Gold*, whose organic, fair-trade coffee would no longer have a market outside their communities, or to the sustainable and fair-trade collectives in Central and South America, which are exporting goods, foods, and clothes to the north. These collectives are helping many people who would likely go out of business if their products were only purchased locally. Of course, we need to pay attention to what happens when a commodity, such as the high-protein grain quinoa grown in poorer countries becomes desirable in richer countries, raising the price so that many people in the countries where it's grown can no longer afford it, and to how disruptions in our complex global supply chain can cause significant harm in communities that are reliant on far removed systems they cannot control (as became apparent during the COVID pandemic). These examples point to the importance of recognizing the complexity of problems and interconnected systems and avoiding oversimplified answers.

Too often the phrase "local economy" is associated with small, equitable, sustainable, and humane, and "global economy" with big, impersonal, and destructive. Yet, there are local companies that are exploitative and cruel (e.g., plenty of pig farms that treat animals inhumanely and cause terrible pollution). There are also many overseas companies that are sustainable and equitable (e.g., plenty of fair-trade cooperative farms).

The localization *versus* globalization argument steers us away from more nuanced choices that arise when we bring a solutionary lens that asks us to examine problems, and the systems that perpetuate them, directly.[26] In other words, we can learn to recognize the positives from both localization and globalization rather than pit them against one another.

If, for example, our primary agricultural problems lie in the following issues, we can and should address these directly and systemically.

- monoculture farms
- poisonous chemicals
- fertilizer run-off creating ocean dead zones
- rampant antibiotic use in farmed animals accelerating antibiotic resistance
- fuel-, water-, land-, and grain-intensive animal agriculture
- exploitation of farm workers and those employed in slaughterhouses
- cruelty to animals
- habitat destruction and soil erosion caused by inefficient food production

Thus, we may find that fair-trade, sustainable, plant-, cell-, and microbial-based food production are meaningful alternatives that shift the economics of agriculture away from exploitation and abuse without closing markets between north and south, east and west, or in the United States between the fertile heartland, citrus-bearing Florida, California (where just about everything grows), and everywhere else.

I'm happy that Maine produces blueberries, potatoes, and lumber for people who live far away from us—although I would like it to do so without toxic pesticides and clear-cutting—and I'm also happy that I can live in Maine and still drink tea and eat avocados produced far away from me.

Global trade currently relies on the use of fossil fuels to transport crops and products across the planet, but as Michael Berners-Lee points out in his carbon footprint assessment of products and foods in his book, *How Bad Are Bananas?*, local doesn't necessarily mean less carbon intensive. His analysis reveals that bananas transported to Northern Europe from equatorial regions in Africa use a small fraction of the fuel needed for the hothouse tomatoes that are grown next door to him in England. And local beef in the United States has bigger global warming impacts than protein-rich legumes transported across the country.[27] Ironically, the energy it takes for local farmers to drive their many pickup trucks to a farmers' market often exceeds the carbon footprint of one semi bringing sustainably produced food from further away.[28] And regardless of whether we rely on locally or globally produced foods and goods, we're going to have to shift to clean energy systems and replace fossil fuels. Once we have made this shift, one of the strongest arguments against global trade will evaporate.

This is all to say that a solutionary lens is not static. It is open to identifying new ideas and ways to transform systems, rarely lands in absolutes, and is always on the lookout for better answers.

———

An either/or lens isn't just a problem in terms of obvious polarization. It can emerge even in situations where people are ostensibly "on the same side" but disagree about tactics. For example, consider this quote from Senator Bernie Sanders printed in the January 2018 issue of *The Sun* magazine:

> Real change never takes place from the top on down. It always takes place from the bottom on up. It takes place when ordinary people, by the millions, are prepared to stand up and fight for justice. That's what the history of the trade-union movement is about. That's what the history of the women's movement is about. That's what the history of the gay-rights movement is about. That's what the history of the environmental movement is about. That's what any serious movement for justice is about.

You may not be surprised that my response to reading this was, "yes, and...."

Real change happens in many ways, not just one. Sometimes change is, indeed, primarily bottom-up, as in the women's suffrage and labor movements. Sometimes it's primarily top-down, as in the ban on chlorofluorocarbons (CFCs), which occurred when scientists discovered that CFCs were creating a hole in the ozone layer, and diplomats adopted the Montreal Protocol to phase out these chemicals. Sometimes change comes through more sustainable technologies and innovations that replace more destructive ones.

I write this as someone who will continue to educate about and advocate for environmental, animal, and human rights protections and policies, but I won't be suggesting that there's only one approach to creating positive societal transformations. We can each learn to identify the particular ways in which we want to become a solutionary who utilizes our talents, skills, and knowledge to make positive shifts happen. Some of us will work to gain political and economic support for better systems. Some will be engaged in trying to transform destructive and inhumane policies. Some will become traditional bottom-up activists agitating for change. Some will set new precedents within the legal system that have powerful top-down effects. Some will develop more sustainable and humane technologies and inventions. Some will shift mindsets and beliefs through education. But my hope is we will all be disinclined to accept statements like "real change *never* takes place" or "*always* takes place" through certain means. Social change is more likely to occur through a combination of strategic bottom-up activism, social businesses and innovations, top-down policy measures from experts and those in positions of power, and educational initiatives that shift perspectives. This means that forming coalitions and collaborating across various sectors of society can speed the process.

We mustn't forget that real and significant societal changes happen all the time, and not necessarily for the better. These changes often occur through the impacts of unexamined societal systems that have become entrenched over decades. For example, how did obesity and type 2 diabetes become so prevalent among children in the United States over the past several decades, disproportionately affecting kids living in poverty?

Industrial agriculture, the Farm Bill, corporate lobbyists, and taxpayer subsidies have made the foods that contribute most significantly to these health problems—refined carbohydrates, fast food, certain kinds of meat, sugary beverages, and junk food—low in price by externalizing the true costs, while fresh fruits and vegetables remain costly because they are not subsidized.[29] Many public school cafeterias have also become the dumping ground for foods that aren't healthful, accustoming children to diets that may harm them. Couple these food system problems with an advertising and legal system that permits ads for unhealthy foods that target children, an educational system that has reduced time for fitness and outdoor play, and a media system with enticing screens that lead to inactivity, and you have a recipe for increased incidence of obesity and type 2 diabetes among children. Hardly a bottom-up change in our society!

How will obesity and type 2 diabetes be solved? We'll look at potential leverage points and solutions to address this problem in chapter 5, and the answers will include a combination of top-down, bottom-up, legislation-determined, education-influenced, and policy-change initiatives.

Solutionary = Next-level Changemaker
Solutionaries take problem-solving to the next level

At the beginning of this book is the definition of the word "solutionary." It includes three noun definitions and two adjective definitions. The first noun definition is this:

> A person who identifies inhumane, unjust, and/or unsustainable societal systems and then develops solutions to transform them so that they do the most good and least harm for people, animals, and the environment.

Embedded in this definition is an ethical imperative. One can solve an engineering problem in order to dam a river or blow up a mountaintop for coal removal, but that does not make one a solutionary. Solutionaries take problem-solving to the next level by ensuring that their solutions do the most good and least harm for everyone: people, animals, and the environment.

Including animals is a distinguishing feature of the term solutionary, but which animals exactly? "Animals" is a big category that encompasses mammals, birds, fishes, reptiles, amphibians, and invertebrates. A commitment to doing the most good and least harm for animals does not mean that all animals carry equal weight when striving to find answers to problems that may impact multiple species. Animal sentience differs between species, and sentience matters. If an animal has a rudimentary (or no) brain and is unlikely to be able to suffer, a solutionary will weigh "harm" differently for that animal than for those animals who are clearly able to experience pain and suffering. Solutionaries will certainly give the benefit of the doubt when there are uncertainties about the capacity for pain, and will always strive to avoid causing harm to any species if they can, but they will seek to maximize the overall good and minimize the overall harm by taking into account the degree of suffering that the animals in question are capable of experiencing. They will, for example, consider tapeworm medication an ethical solution for an infected dog.

Solutionaries take humanitarianism to the next level

There's an oft-told parable about a child rescuing beached starfish by throwing them back into the sea. A pragmatic adult walks by and tells the child that given the thousands of starfish on the shore, throwing them one by one into the ocean can't possibly make a difference. Tossing a starfish back into the water, the child responds, "I made a difference for that one."

This story is meant to serve as a reminder that doing *something* to help matters, which is why if solutionaries encountered thousands of starfish on the shore, they would surely throw some of them back into the ocean. But solutionaries would go further. They would also ask, "What caused the beaching of these animals?" Assuming the beaching wasn't a natural phenomenon, they would investigate to find out the answer and try to address the problem at its source so that next week, next month, and next year, starfish would not be dying on the shores.

It's not uncommon for people to conflate humanitarian and solutionary actions, but they are not the same. Volunteering to resettle refugees fleeing war, sending money to a region that's been decimated by wildfires, or donating blankets to a homeless shelter are humanitarian efforts. They are meant to directly alleviate the symptoms and impacts of an underlying problem. They aren't oriented toward *solving* the problems of war, climate change, or poverty.

Humanitarian efforts are essential. When there are people and animals in need, humanitarians relieve suffering. With that said, our time and resources are limited. If we are *only* humanitarians, we will face never-ending and potentially escalating problems. We must balance our limited time and resources with the imperative to be solutionaries who investigate the root and systemic causes of problems and devise solutions so that these problems cease to exist. This is not an either/or but a "both, and." Solutionaries take humanitarianism to the next level.

At the Institute for Humane Education, we have developed the following rubric to evaluate the "solutionariness" of a solution so that as we work to develop solutions to problems we are better able to distinguish between our humanitarian and solutionary efforts, as well as between solutions that have unintended negative consequences and those that do the most good and least harm for everyone impacted. This rubric isn't meant to discourage humanitarian efforts but rather to clarify the solutionariness of solutions.

EMERGING	DEVELOPING	SOLUTIONARY	MOST SOLUTIONARY
The solution, while well-intentioned, does not yet address root and/or systemic causes (and may produce unintended negative consequences to people, animals, or the environment).	The solution addresses root and/or systemic causes but produces unintended negative consequences to people, animals, or the environment.	The solution addresses root and/or systemic causes and strives not to produce unintended negative consequences to people, animals, or the environment.	The solution **significantly and strategically** addresses root and/or systemic causes and does not harm people, animals, or the environment.

Fig 1.1: Solutionary Rubric. CREDIT: INSTITUTE FOR HUMANE EDUCATION

In 2015, a TV report highlighted the good work of a man who wanted to solve the problems of food waste and hunger simultaneously. His idea was to create a nonprofit that engaged the efforts of volunteers to bring food that would otherwise be thrown out by restaurants to hungry people. Soon he had built a thriving program with many volunteers transporting food from restaurants to soup kitchens and food pantries.

Based on the rubric above, is this solution Emerging? Developing? Solutionary? Most Solutionary?

While the solution certainly alleviates some local food waste problems and helps many individuals, does it address the systems that perpetuate hunger and/or the systems that perpetuate food waste? Is it a scalable solution? Would it be feasible for volunteers to transport the excess food produced and wasted into the hands of all people living in hunger? And if such scalability succeeded, might that potentially entrench the systems that created the inequity and food waste to begin with? Would the solution solve the primary cause of hunger, which is poverty and lack of access to affordable, nutritious food?

In 2018, I spoke at a conference in New York City, and I showed the TV clip of this man and his volunteers and asked the audience to consider where the solution fell on the solutionary scale. One of the people in the audience was a volunteer at a food pantry that was the recipient of this nonprofit's efforts. I was eager to hear her thoughts from her personal experience. She told us that they sometimes had so much food delivered that they were unable to distribute it and had to dispose of it themselves. Thus, there were times when volunteers were transporting food from restaurants to food pantries, only to have it thrown away by other volunteers. Once again, I am not suggesting that we stop supporting such efforts, which are helping hungry people and reducing the disposal of perfectly good food. What I am suggesting is that we simultaneously work to devise ever more solutionary solutions to address these issues systemically in order to bring our work to the next level.

I'm also not suggesting that assessing solutions on the solutionary scale is like math. There is rarely one "right answer." Opinions will differ, but learning how to carefully assess solutions is important if we want to have the biggest impact we can.

Solutionaries take problem-identification to the next level

Whenever we hear about a problem such as food waste, it's also import-ant to investigate its full implications by asking deeper questions: What food is wasted exactly? When? Where? How? Why?

It's estimated that 30-40% of food in the United States is thrown out—a travesty when you consider all the people who don't have enough food to eat. Yet when we hear reports about food waste, it's usually only about this one aspect of waste. What's rarely discussed is the much great-er loss that occurs in the inherently inefficient production of certain foods, especially meat, dairy, and eggs. The vast majority of soybeans, corn, and oats grown for food in the United States is fed to animals, and the conver-sion rate of crops fed to animals to the meat, dairy, and eggs produced is very poor. It can take many pounds of legumes and grains fed to an animal to produce a single pound of meat, milk, or eggs. And not only are we wasting food through the digestive systems of animals (who then create pollution through their copious waste that exceeds our capacity to use as fertilizer), we're also wasting fresh water, and using excess commercial fertilizers and pesticides, while simultaneously depleting precious top-soil, without which we're hard-pressed to grow anything. Put bluntly, we are despoiling the environment by raising animals to eat rather than by eating plants directly.

In other words, food waste is more complicated than we might initial-ly realize. We need to look further than what's thrown away by restaurants that can't always accurately predict what will be ordered; supermarkets that dispose of produce that doesn't "look" good, as well as products with expiration dates that don't result in any actual danger if those dates pass by days or even weeks; large-scale farms whose nonuniform-sized pro-duce has no market; and consumers whose food goes bad in the back of the fridge, or who throw out food from their plates.

This deeper and solutionary-focused investigation of complex chal-lenges takes problem-identification to the next level.

Solutionaries take activism to the next level

Solutionaries sometimes identify as activists, working as they do to bring about social change and intervene in systems that cause harm, but not all activists are solutionaries. While there are many definitions of "activist," activism is commonly associated with protests, civil disobedience, and direct action campaigns.

I've attended many protests, marches, and rallies, and to the degree that they have been organized with meaningful goals in mind, draw attention to problems, and maintain a focus on building energy and momentum for well-articulated actions and changes to the law, they can be very significant levers for change. They also motivate participants to engage in lobbying legislators, influencing corporations, educating community members, and shifting policies.

For example, the 1963 Civil Rights March in Washington, DC, attended by a quarter of a million people, was highly influential in galvanizing efforts to pass civil rights legislation. One of the organizers of and speakers at the march, A. Philip Randolph, was clear about the march's ultimate goal when he closed his speech with the promise that "we here today are only the first wave. When we leave, it will be to carry the civil rights revolution home with us into every nook and cranny of the land, and we shall return again and again to Washington in ever-growing numbers until total freedom is ours."[30] Just over ten months later, the Civil Rights Act was passed by Congress, one of the critical steps in an ongoing process to build a racially just society.

With that said, there are times when protests and rallies devolve into shouting, name-calling, and sometimes violence, and this can lead non-activists—who may only see the worst behaviors captured by media that consistently seek to highlight conflict—to reject the activists' important goals because of the method with which they are being pursued and how their message is being portrayed. When this happens, those positive goals become undermined.

The same problems can arise with acts of civil disobedience. Sometimes, such actions can be very effective, gaining media attention for injustices and setting the stage for legal and policy changes. At other times, if these actions have negative impacts on others, for example, by blockading a roadway during rush hour to protest perceived inaction on climate change, they can set back achievement of the activists' goals by creating ill will and backlash.[31]

When solutionary-focused activists experience frustration and anger, as they often do, they strive to vent those feelings in ways that don't undermine their objectives. This can be as simple as expressing pent-up emotions with friends and colleagues to get their frustrations off their chest privately. If they know they have this kind of support, they are often better able to contain their negative emotions in public, even in highly challenging situations where people are insulting, goading, or trying to rile them up. For those who are drawn to "street activism," it can be very helpful to do role-plays and gain practice in order to take activism to the next level and be better prepared for times where emotions may flare.

When I was in my twenties, with fire in the belly to address cruelty and suffering, I sometimes joined leafleting efforts. Armed with my leaflets, I was friendly to passersby as I offered them one of my fliers. I was usually ignored, sometimes sneered at, and on one occasion told to "get a life." When people dropped the leaflet I'd given them on the sidewalk after a quick glance, I could feel my blood boil. Not only didn't they care enough to read the flier, they were now littering! Eventually I realized that leafleting was not my solutionary way because I was not good at managing my frustrations and being a solutionary in situations that triggered my anger. I needed to (and did) find a better solutionary path for myself. But for others with a calmer, more equanimous temperament, leafleting can be a way to educate the public as a solutionary, provided the leaflet provides accurate information and clear, positive steps readers of the leaflet can take to make a difference.

I have a friend, Kim Korona, an extraordinary humane educator who has been an activist since high school, when she created her first petition to address income inequality and support fair wages. Kim has participated in many traditional forms of activism such as leafleting, canvassing, and attending rallies, along with creative forms of activism such as change-oriented dance and theater. She has addressed international and national issues as well as local problems, as when she organized the tenants in her building in New York City to compel the owner to fix the boiler that was emitting toxic fumes and to remove the black mold in the apartments that were making tenants ill. Kim even brought activism to her wedding by providing postcards for guests to sign to repeal the

Defense of Marriage Act (DOMA). It pained Kim that while she could marry her husband, gay and lesbian couples could not, so she made her wedding day an opportunity to engage friends and family in efforts to extend marriage equality, a problem that has since been solved through the work of people like Kim.

Kim is one of the kindest people I know. While she periodically feels sad, she rarely gets angry at people, and her warmth draws people to learn from her. She's a solutionary in so many aspects of her life, including in her activism.

Chapter 2:

MOST GOOD, LEAST HARM (MOGO)

Would You Kill a Cousin for a Full Head of Hair?

IN SEPTEMBER 2022, I attended a screening of the Manhattan Short Film Festival. After watching ten films, I and the other audience members voted for the one we thought should win. I voted for Álvaro Carmona's *The Treatment*.[32] In this provocative film, a bald man and his presumed spouse visit a treatment center for baldness. Meeting with a representative of "the treatment," which consists of a $6,000 pill that permanently ensures a full head of hair, the couple learns that there is a side effect. Within a few days, a cousin of the man will die. But the representative is quick to assure the client that it might be a second cousin he sees only at an occasional wedding.

As one would expect, the couple is disbelieving and horrified, but the representative, who shares a photo of his own baldness before the treatment, offers his personal head as a tactile example of what the client will experience in perpetuity if he takes the pill. The couple strokes his hair, and we witness their resolve to resist the treatment weakening. The representative reminds them that people die all the time.

The couple leaves, and it seems they are actually considering the treatment. Then, in the lobby, they run into one of the man's (bald) cousins whom they haven't seen since a long-ago wedding. He is arriving for his own meeting with the representative. And so ends the film.

The premise of *The Treatment* is ridiculous of course, but it is also a brilliant way of telling an extreme version of the story of our everyday lives. Like the bald man in *The Treatment*, people with means regularly spend significant amounts of money on things that they believe will improve their lives, whether their physical appearance (e.g., cosmetics and high-end clothing), their pleasure (e.g., far-flung vacations and costly forms of entertainment), their status (e.g., jewels and luxury cars), or simply their preferences (e.g., a purebred dog).

Most people don't consider these choices as having an ethical component and certainly not one as stark as that described in *The Treatment*, but they are similar to the film's obviously unethical choice because they are all examples of putting the fulfillment of our desires above others' lives. The truth is that for me writing this and for most people reading this, we cause a lot of harm through our choices but are rarely encouraged to reflect upon our complicity.

For example, many cosmetics are tested on animals who are killed solely for our vanity. Our flights to go on vacation are a significant contributor to climate change, and until we replace fossil fuels with clean energy sources, they will remain so. The jewelry we buy may carry a trail of environmental destruction and the exploitation of miners. When we purchase a puppy from a breeder or pet shop, there's a dog in a shelter who didn't get a home and may soon be killed for lack of space.

The Treatment only appears far-fetched because the man is told that someone in his extended family will die so that he can have a full head of hair, but the reality is that many someones in our global family—human and nonhuman—die all the time because of our choices. While it can be uncomfortable to recognize this truth, the realization that our choices can do more good and less harm can be empowering and liberating.

The MOGO Principle

"Most good, least harm" isn't simply the ethical imperative embedded in the solutionary process; it is also a principle by which to make personal choices. I refer to it as the MOGO Principle (short for MOst GOod), and it takes the universally embraced Golden Rule, to do unto others as we would have them do unto us, and puts it into practice in a globalized world in which our everyday choices have far-reaching impacts.

Given that virtually every product we buy, item of clothing we wear, form of energy and transportation we use, and morsel of food we put in our mouths are part of intricate systems that impact not only our own lives but also other people, animals, and ecosystems across the planet,

MOGO choice-making can be challenging. But even though we cannot fully extricate ourselves from systems that cause harm, we can still endeavor to make personal decisions that are MOGO.

While at first this might sound like an exhausting effort amidst busy lives, MOGO can and does lead to meaning and happiness. There are myriad choices we can make that will bring us pleasure, or better yet, joy, that not only minimize unintended negative consequences but which also contribute to a better world.

When I was writing my book *Most Good, Least Harm* I asked hundreds of people what brought them joy. I knew that few people would pursue a MOGO life if doing so felt like endless deprivation or guilt, so I wanted to discover whether choosing MOGO was compatible with personal happiness. No one told me that stuff (clothing, jewelry, or other purchased objects) brought them joy. Almost everyone talked about being with loved ones—both humans and animals—and many mentioned experiences in nature. There were also a number of people who wrote about helping others and working for a cause greater than themselves. It was striking how many people named service as their primary path to joy.

The MOGO principle doesn't ask us to make any specific choices; it simply asks us to reflect upon the effects of our choices so that when we make decisions, we are considering their impacts. The more conscious we are and the more we are able to make choices aligned with our values, the less inner conflict we are likely to experience and the greater our potential for inner peace. (You'll find a MOGO Questionnaire in the appendix to help you introspect in this way.)

Do Our Personal Choices Really Matter?

In the scheme of things, no number of bike rides instead of car rides or cups of fair-trade, shade-grown coffee instead of conventional coffee is going to end injustice, cruelty, and environmental degradation, so one might argue (and many do) that our personal choices don't add up to much. To which I respond, "yes, and...."

The *collective* efforts of individuals matter quite a bit. Together, our choices add up to new forms of production that are less toxic, new testing protocols that aren't cruel to animals, new forms of agriculture that are regenerative and humane, to name just a few examples. Within a capitalist system, if there isn't demand from people who want products and foods that cause less harm, these new products and foods won't get produced. And within a democracy, if there isn't outcry from people who contact their legislators and vote, new laws and regulations that support more equitable, sustainable, and humane systems are less likely to be enacted.[33]

We mustn't underestimate the power of either our political vote or our dollar, which is our economic vote. Just as our votes choose our legislators and members of our school boards, the money we spend chooses the products, foods, and services available to us. Our personal choices also matter because they represent our integrity. If we don't walk our talk, why should anyone listen to us?

Why the Superlative?

I've been asked why the MOGO principle isn't "more good, less harm" rather than "most good, least harm." To examine one's daily choices—from food, clothing, products, energy consumption, transportation, participation in citizenship, volunteerism, charitable giving, et cetera—and make sure to do the *most* good and the *least* harm could seem overwhelming, but that's not the purpose of the superlative.

The reason why it's worth striving to discover what does the *most* good and the *least* harm is because the act of identifying "most" and "least" matters. We can't develop truly MOGO systems and products if we aren't able to clarify what these would even be. So by all means, do more good and less harm as you are able, but please don't give up on discovering what it would mean to do the most good and the least harm.

The 3 I's

To support your MOGO decision-making, I invite you to embrace what I call the 3 I's of Inquiry, Introspection, and Integrity (which will complement and support the four phases of the solutionary process—Identify, Investigate, Innovate, and Implement—that we'll get to in chapter 5).

Inquiry

We cannot do more good and less harm, let alone the most good and least harm, if we don't endeavor to deeply understand our impacts in the world. For example, perhaps you're someone who wants to be sure that your food choices don't contribute to animal cruelty, but you really don't know all that much about animal agricultural practices. You know that animals are killed for meat, of course, and you suspect there may be suffering involved, so perhaps you decide to limit your meat consumption. But since dairy and eggs require a living animal to produce them, you might imagine that these foods don't cause harm to animals, since the cows and chickens aren't killed to produce them.

To be sure, you decide to inquire. What will you discover?

Eggs

The norm in the egg industry is to cram as many hens as possible into cages, after cutting off up to half of their sensitive, nerve-infused beaks—without painkillers or anesthesia—to prevent the stronger from killing the weaker hens by pecking them to death under such confined conditions. There the hens will live their whole lives, breathing the ammonia from their accumulated waste, standing on a sloped wire cage that allows their eggs to roll onto a conveyor belt and their excrement to fall through the spaces between the wires, never able to stretch a wing, take a dust bath, roost, feel the sun, or breathe fresh air. When their egg production wanes after about a year, they will be grabbed out of these cages by their legs, stuffed into transport crates, and carted off to the slaughterhouse to be killed.

The photo below is one that I took when I brought a group of students to visit one of the largest egg producers on the east coast of the United States. This Pennsylvania facility provided eggs all the way up to Maine and all the way down to Florida. There were half a million birds crushed together into floor-to-ceiling cages like these. Underneath their cages was a huge pit of their waste. The stench was overwhelming, but according to our guide at the facility, the waste would not be cleaned out even once during their confinement. Only after the hens were sent off to be killed for the soup factory across the river would the facility be cleaned in preparation for the next batch of hens.

Fig: 2.1: Egg-laying hens crammed into a typical "battery cage." CREDIT: ZOE WEIL

There were several brands that purchased their eggs from this factory, and each had their own egg cartons. Below is a photo of one of the cartons, which they let us take after our tour. It suggests a very different kind of "farm," but no laws prevented this company from misleading the consumer about the conditions under which the hens were raised.

Fig: 2.2: Egg carton from the egg facility above. CREDIT: ZOE WEIL

Our inquiry has brought us this far, which is farther than most people will likely get in their knowledge about the eggs they consume. But what else might we want to know?

We might want to ask where these hens came from, and what happened to the male chicks who hatched in the hatchery that supplied the hens to this facility. We know that male chickens don't lay eggs and therefore won't be of any use to the egg industry, so where did they go? It won't take long to learn that the male chicks aren't of use to the meat industry either, because egg-laying chickens aren't bred to be as fast-growing as "broiler" chickens. Typically, the male chicks will either be thrown alive into the trash and crushed by the chicks thrown on top of them or tossed (again, alive) into grinding machines to be ground up as feed for other animals or used as fertilizer. This is a shocking reality to discover.

Maybe you already knew that there was cruelty involved in the egg industry, so you have been choosing eggs with cartons that read "cage-free" or "free-range." But it's worth inquiring about these labels, too. Do they really mean that no cruelty or suffering was involved?

While "cage-free" means that the hens won't be in cages during egg production, it doesn't mean they will be outdoors, able to roost, keep their beaks intact, or be provided with enough space for a humane life. And while "free-range" does mean that the hens will spend *some* time outdoors, there is no regulation that ensures their outdoor time will be frequent or provide much space at all. So, while many fast-food restaurants, food companies, and even some states are moving toward "cage-free" egg production—which is a significant and welcome improvement—this doesn't mean that the eggs were produced without animal suffering.

There are other labels some companies are able to secure because they treat their hens well and provide adequate outdoor space and places to roost, but none of these labels ensure that the chicks come from hatcheries that treat the males humanely or that the hens will live out their natural lifespans in peace and not wind up crammed into cages to be trucked to slaughterhouses. In other words, the larger system is likely to be inhumane.

Dairy

What about milk? Growing up I never considered why a cow would produce milk for people. I assumed that cows spontaneously produced milk and farmers sat by their sides and relieved them of the milk that would fill their udders. That's what the drawings in picture books depicted, and I was told we were doing the cows a favor because they needed to be milked. I didn't give this process a second thought.

But cows don't spontaneously produce milk. Like all mammals, they produce milk to feed their own babies, and to obtain cow's milk for ourselves, we artificially inseminate cows and then take their calves away, usually within a day. After essentially kidnapping their offspring, for whom the cows will sometimes bellow out for days, we hook these cows up to milking machines.

We breed dairy cows to produce more and more milk and often give them hormones to boost their milk production even further, which causes their udders to become huge and distended. The typical dairy cow in the United States is forced to produce six to seven times the amount of milk she would normally produce to feed her own calf. This leads to mastitis, a painful udder infection, in 20–50% of US dairy cows, necessitating antibiotic treatment.[34] Within months of giving birth, she'll be inseminated and forced to bear another calf, who will be taken away yet again. The cycle continues until she is so spent—and often lame—that she is sent off to slaughter, usually to become hamburger.

And what of her male offspring? Like male chicks in the egg industry, male calves are of no use to the dairy industry,[35] and about 15–20% of them wind up in veal production, either killed immediately or raised in extreme confinement for high-end veal, with the rest raised for beef. When I learned about calf confinement in veal production, I wanted to see it for myself, and so I wrote to the Pennsylvania Veal Association (PVA), requesting a tour for my students. The PVA declined to provide a tour, but they did send me pamphlets and a video to share with my class. I showed my students the thirty-minute video, which depicted people interviewed after a tour of a veal facility with only a minute or so in which we got to see any footage of the calves. After watching the video, the students wrote letters to the PVA. Many of them asked why they couldn't see a veal farm for themselves. One year later, I got a call from a farmer producing veal in a confinement facility. They had finally agreed to give my students and me a tour.

When we arrived, we were brought into a barn with rows of calves chained at the neck in tiny stalls barely bigger than their bodies. Although seemingly clean (perhaps spruced up for our visit), it was difficult to breathe because of the foul smell. The calves could take a single step backwards or forwards, but that was the limit of their mobility. The reason they were confined was so that they couldn't exercise, which would cause their muscles to develop and make their flesh less tender, a preference consumers have been taught to desire. The calves were desperate to suckle and latched onto our fingers to do just that, though obviously no milk was forthcoming. The students and I felt so sad. Not only were we witnessing what we perceived as terribly inhumane treatment, we also knew that after four months, these calves would be forced by electric prods to walk on atrophied legs onto the trucks that would take them to slaughter.

Once we learn that all these practices are the norm in the dairy industry, we come to realize there may be even more suffering involved in milk production than in the beef industry. If we were limiting our meat consumption while eating dairy to diminish the harm to animals in our diet, learning this is quite a wakeup call.

So perhaps we seek out different dairy products, labeled organic. But organic doesn't necessarily mean humane. Organic means that the cows generally eat feed produced without fertilizers or pesticides, have some access to pasture, don't receive supplemental hormones, and aren't given antibiotics. It doesn't mean that the calves weren't taken away from their mothers at birth, that some of the male calves weren't raised in cruel confinement for veal, and that their mothers won't be forced to endure annual pregnancies and milking until they are utterly depleted and even lame. Like other dairy cows, they will almost always wind up at the slaughterhouse, too.

So far, I've just touched the surface of the animal suffering involved in egg and dairy production, and there are other questions to inquire about as well, such as:

- Why do we consume the milk of another species?
- Why do we consume milk products long past when we were weaned as babies or toddlers?
- Are dairy products actually healthful?
- What is transport for the animals like, especially in the heat of summer and cold of winter?

- What are the conditions like in slaughterhouses, both for the animals and the people who work in them?[36]
- What are the human health and environmental impacts of the waste produced by dairy cows, and who is most affected by it?

Why have I spent several pages of this book, in the section about inquiry, talking about eggs and dairy? The reason is because eggs and dairy products are ubiquitous, part of many people's daily lives, and they provide an example of complex systems in which we may take part without having any idea about the far-reaching impacts of those systems. We think we know, but we may not. And we may not inquire because:

- It's time-consuming to conduct research to ascertain the impacts of our choices. Since it would be impossible to examine the impact of everything we choose, we may choose to avoid seeking out any information at all.
- We're inclined to trust and believe the labels that suggest a product meets ethical standards, even if those labels have little regulation behind them. We prefer to equate "organic" with "humane," "cage-free" with "outdoors and spacious," and "humane" with "humane throughout the entire system of production" rather than look too deeply and discover we've been duped.
- We want to be compassionate, responsible people. To commit to inquiry might mean we learn that we are not as ethical as we'd like to be. We may prefer not to know rather than be conscious of the fact that we are allowing our desires to eclipse our values.

With that said, here's why it's such a meaningful thing to do and why having inquiry become a default mindset is truly valuable:

- Inquiry is a direct result of our innate curiosity and leads to learning, which is inherently interesting and engaging. Learning also leads to new opportunities and connections.

- Inquiry results in more nuanced thinking, perspective-taking, and successful problem-solving, all of which lead to healthier societies.
- We can't really live with integrity if we aren't willing to inquire about the impacts of our actions, and integrity, which we'll get to shortly, matters.

What could inquiry look like in your daily life? Let's say you want a new shirt. Most of the time, when we want something, the only question we ask ourselves is: Can I afford it? Embracing the MOGO principle means asking other questions too, such as:

- Do I need another shirt?
- Am I willing to learn about the impacts of a potential shirt I might acquire and choose one that aligns with my values?
- Does it have to be new? If yes:
  - Can I find a shirt from a company that is committed to fair labor practices, production that uses sustainable materials and environmentally friendly dyes, and produces clothing that lasts?
  - Can I find a shirt produced by a fair-trade collective in a country where such production is helping people break out of poverty or one produced locally so that I'm supporting my own community?
- Does it have to be new? If no:
  - Do I want to support a chain thrift shop, a locally owned thrift shop, or a nonprofit thrift shop that donates to a charity I believe in?
  - Do I want to host a clothing swap with friends?

While at first this inquiry process could seem daunting (and impossible to bring to every purchase we make), questions like these can become second nature, raising our awareness and informing our decisions. With that said, it's important to take a balanced approach to this process, recognizing what is and isn't realistic given our time, resources, and support systems. Which leads us to the second I: introspection.

Introspection

As you practice inquiry and learn more about the impacts of your choices, the next step is to self-reflect. What new and different choices might you want to make? What's feasible within the constraints of your finances and your family? What's motivating you to make certain choices? What's holding you back? What help do you need to make choices more aligned with your values, and where can you get it?

Be compassionate with yourself during this process. You may discover qualities that are uncomfortable to acknowledge (e.g., you may not be willing to give up something you like even though you've learned it causes significant harm or suffering). You'll also likely discover other qualities that are wonderful to realize (e.g., you're willing to make other choices you never imagined you'd make, and you feel really good about your willingness to learn, grow, and change).

Long ago, when I introspected about my clothing purchases, I came to the conclusion that I could bypass the inquiry questions as long as I bought used clothes, since regardless of their original production, my dollars wouldn't be contributing to harm since I was essentially recycling clothing. Buying used clothes also meant that I saved lots of money, as well as time that I might have spent researching which companies I wanted to support.

But eventually I had to ask myself a deeper question: Why are there so many thrift stores with so many new and barely worn clothes? The truth is that the larger "fast fashion" system was making it possible for me to make what I considered to be MOGO choices by buying used clothing, but if we successfully changed the larger system, I might not have an endless supply of options at thrift shops. My belief that I could bypass inquiry by purchasing used clothes was suddenly upended by a new question, and that new question emerged because inquiry had become a default mindset.

Through introspection, I came to realize what I imagine is obvious to you already: it's impossible to do all good and no harm. This realization has helped me become less judgmental of both myself and others. As I recognize my own fallibility and the complexity of doing the most good and least harm in a globalized world, I am less inclined to blame and shame and more inclined to strive so all may thrive.

A couple of days before beginning to write this chapter, I was driving behind a very slow truck that was traveling way under the speed limit. I needed to get back to work and was frustrated by the driver. As the truck slowed down to take the same turn I was going to take, I was even more frustrated. Now I would be behind him even longer. He slowed to a crawl to make the turn. Suddenly I noticed a chipmunk dart out in front of the truck and then saw the little animal crushed under the truck's tires.

I felt nauseated. I was so upset. I was also angry. Surely the driver of that truck—going so very slowly—could have put on the brakes to avoid killing the chipmunk. I wanted to unsee that death and to confront the driver who, to me, lacked compassion.

Only later—introspecting—did I come to have some disconcerting thoughts. It's likely that given the speed of the darting animal, he couldn't react quickly enough (assuming he even saw the chipmunk). He, too, might have felt sick to his stomach if he'd seen that he killed the animal. It's also possible that because I was riding the truck's tail in my impatience, the driver didn't put on the brakes because I was too close to him. Perhaps if I'd been further away, he would have braked to avoid killing the chipmunk. That chipmunk might have died because of me. Not likely, but possible.

I didn't like having this realization, but it was important. By introspecting I opened up to the possibility of being a different—and better—version of myself: more honest, more patient, more self-aware, more compassionate, and less judgmental. If I can see my role and responsibility in causing harm and not assume that others are irresponsible and uncaring, I am more likely to be able to build the bridges that will need to be built for collaborative solutionary thinking and action.

Integrity

Mahatma Gandhi was once asked by a reporter, "What is your message?" Gandhi had taken a vow of silence that day, so in response he jotted down on a piece of paper, "My life is my message." The first time I heard this story, I was struck by its universality. If Gandhi's life was his message, I realized that meant that my life was my message. Each person's life is their message, whether we like it or not. So the question I had to ask myself was whether or not I was living the message I most wanted to live. Or, more simply, was I living with integrity?

In sum, when we inquire, we gain new knowledge. When we introspect, we gain new insight into the path we want to take. Together inquiry and introspection enable us to make choices that allow us to live with integrity. Living with integrity isn't going to improve systems by itself, but again, collectively our efforts to live with integrity and make MOGO choices add up. Plus living with integrity feels great, and its reverse, not so much.

To bring us back to the example with which I began this section on the 3 I's, today nearly one third of US hens used in egg production no longer live in cages, and plant-based alternatives to eggs are available in grocery stores across the US. This is a result of tireless animal activists working to pass legislation outlawing caging in several states, food entrepreneurs creating alternatives to eggs, and millions of "dollar votes" cast by consumers who don't want to support animal suffering. While these changes haven't (yet) ended animal cruelty in the industry, they remind us that our choices can and do matter. In terms of dairy products, all you need to do is look on the grocery store shelves to see all the non-dairy milks on the market. Delicious non-dairy yogurts, ice cream, and cheeses are available now, too. While none of these alternatives is perfect, when MOGO choice-making rather than perfection is the goal, we can continually move toward ever more humane and sustainable foods and products. As for veal, demand has declined dramatically from when I took my students to visit that veal production facility in Pennsylvania.

The three I's are not a "how to." They will not give you the "right answer." They do not make it *easy* to do the most good and the least harm, but they make it *possible*. Moreover, the investigative and thinking processes that go into MOGO choice-making are important elements of solutionary thinking and action.

MOGO for Whom?

The MOGO principle is broad by design. Often, we compartmentalize the good we seek to achieve by choosing to help people *or* animals *or* the environment. We may then compartmentalize even more, for example choosing to work for causes that help certain people, or extending efforts on behalf of dogs and cats but not pigs and rats, or engaging in advocacy for a specific environmental issue. There is nothing wrong with this. Narrowing our efforts often enables us to achieve greater success. However, making personal choices and devising solutions to systemic problems without taking everyone into consideration may mean that we are limiting the potential positive impact that we can have and potentially causing unintended harm. Below are some examples to illustrate what I mean.

Which birds?

I love observing and learning about birds, and periodically I attend talks by bird experts. At one such talk, the presenter, an ornithologist, asked the audience, "What is a bird worth?" This provocative question was followed by a slide of an Ibis—a big wading bird with a long, curved beak—and a marquee outside of a southern fast-food restaurant that read: 1 wing Ibis - $1.69, 2 wing Ibis - $2.29.

Audience members gasped.

After a dramatic pause, the ornithologist let us know that this marquee wasn't as it appeared. Ibis really read 1bis, and "bis" was short for biscuit. The wings referred to chicken wings. In other words, you could buy one chicken wing and a biscuit for $1.69 or two chicken wings and a biscuit for $2.29.[37] Many members of the audience laughed, and I heard a collective sigh of relief. I did not laugh, nor did I feel relieved. I was amazed that the ornithologist didn't realize that he had shown us exactly what a bird—a specific bird called a chicken—was worth.

I went up to him after his talk and told him how interesting it was that his slide provided the answer to his question, at least in relation to chickens, who, I pointed out, were birds. He looked at me with a puzzled expression. He didn't seem to understand the point I was making. He quickly turned his attention away from me, unable to recognize this blind spot that sought to protect some species of bird while unconsciously denying the worth of others.

Which sea animals?

Many people who eat tuna fish seek out cans with labels that read "dolphin-safe," which refers to tuna who have been caught without netting dolphins. Fishing for tuna by netting dolphins is a common practice by the industry because tuna often swim under dolphins. Lots of people choose dolphin-safe tuna because they love dolphins and don't want to hurt them. But what about the tuna? Tuna may not be mammals like dolphins, but they can still suffer when they are netted, or hooked and dragged by their sensitive mouths, and then hauled onto ships where they cannot breathe. We do not need to harm and kill them to be happy and healthy. The MOGO principle asks us to consider both tunas and dolphins when we make food choices, rather than just one.

Which people?

When we consider what does the most good and least harm for people, it's important to ask ourselves which people? "People" is a big category. "People" will almost always benefit from choices we make, even ones that are harmful to other people. For example, if someone buys a large new SUV, the people who work at the car dealership will benefit. So will the employees and shareholders at the company that produced the SUV, as well as those who work for and are invested in the companies that supplied the components. Those who are employed in the fossil fuel industry as well as investors in that industry will benefit, too. In fact, lots and lots of people will benefit, and most of these people will not be highly paid CEOs from these companies (though executives will benefit far more than those working on oil rigs or assembling cars).

But does buying a large vehicle do the most good and least harm for the majority of people? Climate change is happening primarily because of our rampant use of fossil fuels, and a warming climate is a particular threat to those living on low-lying islands and coasts that are likely to be submerged as sea level rises. Climate change-caused droughts, fires, storms, and floods can certainly impact all people, but it is those with the fewest resources who generally endure the greatest suffering, and who are least likely to be able to escape or recover. Hurricane Harvey, which caused massive flooding in Houston, Texas, in 2017, displaced more than thirty thousand people, disproportionately affecting those with low incomes.[38] The 2022 floods in Pakistan killed more than twelve hundred people, injured more than twelve thousand, and left more than two million homeless.[39]

Perhaps this example is too easy. Many readers of this book may have already made the choice not to buy a large car, but what about other choices that have a big carbon footprint? When we consider the impacts of our choices on "people," it's important to bring nuance to the MOGO principle and identify not only the extent of harm and good but also on whom. Otherwise, we may find ourselves justifying our choices by pointing out the beneficiaries of our decisions. Since there will almost always be beneficiaries, we need to be honest with ourselves about the bigger impacts.

Make MOGO Choices, But Don't Stop There

I hope you're feeling energized to make MOGO choices, but just in case you're feeling overwhelmed with the challenge of pursuing a truly MOGO life, I'll end this chapter with two suggestions. There is an art to keeping the heat on ourselves in a gentle way, and the outcome of practicing this art is often a refreshing sense of humility coupled with a diminishment of judgmentalness (a topic I'll discuss in the next chapter). To find the sweet spot between being too hard and not hard enough on yourself, I recommend making a commitment to choose one, reasonable-for-you MOGO choice to embrace at a time. When that choice has become your new normal, choose another. You might assess your effort at the start of each month. Sustainable and simple monthly resolutions can easily become new habits. If you sometimes fail to stick with your resolutions, acknowledge the challenges you faced and allow that failure to make you more humble and less judgmental of others. When you succeed, pat yourself on the back and let your success buoy your continued efforts.

The second suggestion is to recognize that MOGO choice-making is a "both, and..." rather than an either/or. We can do our best to make MOGO choices, *and* we can work to change those systems from which we cannot fully divest ourselves through personal decision-making. For example, you may wish to minimize your personal carbon footprint, yet no one reading this book can avoid fossil fuels. They are embedded in every system in which we take part—agriculture, transportation, heating and cooling, construction, production, infrastructure, and technology (e.g., the computer on which I'm writing this book). We can strive to reduce our carbon footprint *and* work to change energy systems. Perhaps you are a white person infuriated by racial injustice while remaining advantaged by systems that have enabled you to enjoy educational, economic, housing, legal, career, health, and other privileges and opportunities that many non-white people have difficulty accessing. You can do your best to become knowledgeable about the ways you may inadvertently perpetuate racism, *and* you can work to change the systems that still perpetuate it.

This leads us to the next chapter in which we'll explore what it means to think like a solutionary and to focus on systems change.

Chapter 3:

THINKING LIKE A SOLUTIONARY

Be Aware of Assumptions and Judgments

M Y HUSBAND, Edwin, and I occasionally visit a remote coastal Maine village on the Canadian border, a couple of hours from where we live. During one of our trips there, we had an experience that caused us to reflect upon how our assumptions, judgments, and personal experiences shape our reactions, thoughts, behaviors, attitudes, and even our ability to comprehend reality.

We were taking a stroll to the shore before dinner when a pale, hunched-over young man suddenly appeared, moving quickly toward us, bundled up on a warm day. About twenty feet away, he caught sight of us and appeared startled. He turned around abruptly, quickened his already fast pace, and rushed back the way he came.

Edwin and I exchanged glances and kept walking. We didn't share what we were each feeling—which was a bit fearful—until later at dinner. Only then did Edwin tell me that when we initially encountered the man, he had instinctively palmed his pocket knife. I admitted that I, too, immediately thought about how to protect myself, secretly imagining using my self-defense training against this presumed potential attacker.

Before revealing those immediate fears and thoughts to one another, however, we continued on our way. When we got to the beach, we saw the man again, way down near the water. Curiosity now replaced fear. We pondered aloud whether the man was high and if paranoia had precipitated his sudden retreat on the trail.

We walked toward the water and then along the beach in the opposite direction from the man, with Edwin periodically glancing over his shoulder to keep an eye on him, though by now he was quite far away.

The tide was coming in, and we were getting hungry, so before long we turned back. Suddenly, Edwin pointed to the man in the distance. He was lying face down on the sand.

I was no longer afraid; nor was I curious. I was *alarmed*. I thought the man might be depressed and planning to let the sea swallow him up. Only later at dinner did I become aware that the previous week's news—during which the media had been reporting the rising incidence of suicide—had primed me to project suicidality onto the man.

I told Edwin I thought we needed to intervene. I began to imagine myself approaching the man, asking if he was all right, and offering to help. I even pictured myself saving his life. Edwin, however, did not perceive the situation as an emergency and didn't relish intervening un- necessarily. He said that it would only be about ten minutes before the tide would reach him and that we should wait. If the man didn't move, then we would intervene. While I didn't like the idea of letting the waves practically lap at this man's body before helping, I reluctantly agreed.

We continued to walk toward him, and all at once I noticed that he resembled two large seaweed- and barnacle-covered rocks. In fact, there was no prone man about to be covered by the rising tide. It had been an optical illusion. The man was no longer even on the beach.

I felt bewildered by how easily I'd been taken in by a mirage, how quickly my emotions had changed, and how thoroughly I'd crafted my little stories, both about the man as well as my own potential to do something vaguely heroic. I'd gone from "he's dangerous" to "he's stoned and paranoid" to "he's suicidal" based on virtually nothing. I'd also gone from "I'm afraid" to "I'm a scrappy fighter" to "I'm a potential hero" in as little time.

I was unnerved by the realization that I had made so many assump- tions and judgments with so little information, but such self-awareness was not new to me. As a humane educator, I've been teaching people for decades to become aware of their assumptions and judgments. One activity I use to do this was developed by my friend and humane edu- cator Melissa Feldman. During the activity, I ask audience members to tell me what assumptions or judgments they would have about me if they passed me on the street carrying a pink-striped Victoria's Secret bag (which I conveniently pull out from behind a desk or podium). I ask the same question holding a robin's-egg blue Tiffany's bag and then a plastic Walmart bag.

My audiences have no shortage of assumptions and judgments based on nothing more than a bag. I've been told I must be rich, sexy, gift-giving, classy, clueless, self-centered, thoughtless, shallow, poor, and so much more.

Becoming aware of how quickly we make assumptions and judgments enables us to challenge ourselves, choose our responses more consciously, and, ultimately, think more clearly so that we can make decisions based on reality, not simply our distorted perceptions. When we realize how easily we can be duped by our own stories, illusions, and projections, we may also be more willing to question how many other assumptions we've made that were never overtly falsified by reality. This, in turn, allows us to be more open-minded, humble, and thoughtful and to better challenge our cognitive biases.

Because by nature we are quick to make assumptions and judgments, and because most of our experiences in the present are interpreted through the lens of past experiences, we won't be able to entirely prevent our reactions and immediate responses. But by doing what Edwin and I did at dinner after our encounter with the man on the beach—deconstructing our immediate reactions, identifying previous experiences that sparked our conclusions, and carefully following the train of thought that led us to our various emotions and actions—each of us can become more practiced at identifying our assumptions and judgments. This will provide greater capacity for and agility with solutionary thinking.

Resist Judgmentalness

Not only is it important to become cognizant of our assumptions and judgements, we also need to resist judgmentalness, which comes all too naturally to many, if not most of us. In our society, judgmentalness is often rewarded, which makes resisting the urge to judge others even harder. For example, the judgier the post, the more likes and reposts it often seems to get. The judgier the pundit, the higher the ratings and the larger the viewership.

But judgmentalness is leading us toward incivility, bullying, and ever more polarization and away from solutionary thinking. I say this as someone who has judged with the best of them, even if I've tried to keep the expression of my judgmentalness within a narrow sphere of close friends and family. Nonetheless, judginess has oozed out despite my best intentions. For example, back in my 20s, I regularly approached people wearing fur with a smile on my face and judginess in my heart as I handed them a polite card explaining the cruelty involved in the production of their coat.

It was only after one woman in a full-length mink came up to me after reading the card and called me out on my hurtful look that I reconsidered. She told me she'd inherited the coat and explained its sentimental value. That didn't change my opinion that wearing fur promotes and endorses animal cruelty, but it did soften my judgmentalness of her personally.

To be clear, there's nothing wrong with judging *actions*. One of the most esteemed professions in the United States is being a judge. Being a good judge requires careful listening, deep reflection, and equanimity in order to determine what consequences should follow destructive, unethical, and illegal acts, and what outcomes are fair and wise in response to conflicts between people. Judges are supposed to bring objectivity, sagacity, and clarity of thought, not judgmentalness, as they weigh their decisions carefully.

To be solutionaries, we, too, need to bring careful, mindful judgment to the challenges before us, while doing our best to avoid judging individuals. We all have our histories and our baggage. We all live with various levels of reactivity, apathy, hurt, denial, and hypocrisy. We're all imperfect. We can consciously choose to cut the person we're inclined to judge some slack, even as we strive to influence them to change the behaviors we believe are worthy of judgment.

To succeed at this effort to temper judgmentalness, it helps to reflect upon how it feels to be judged. You've likely felt the sting of others' judgments. Ask yourself if you really want to add to the potential suffering and pain of someone else by casting judgment on them. Unless the person has wronged you personally, chances are you don't. You might also pay attention to the negative impacts of judgmentalness on yourself and your relationships. There's no doubt that being judgy can be plea-surable, albeit in an unhealthy way. It can create bonds with those who share our judgments. It can, as mentioned above, gain attention and even a following. But does it make you happier or healthier to judge others? To perseverate on their imperfections? To talk ill of someone to a friend and then realize that your friend might be noticing that they, too, could be the object of your judgmentalness if they do something you think is wrong? Now imagine the reverse: What might it be like to accept others with all their imperfections even as you try to influence them to take different actions? Might this be liberating?

For the suggestions above to work, you'll need to introspect about whether you really *want* to be less judgmental. If the answer is yes, pay attention as judgmentalness arises. Notice it's arising and choose to let it go, again and again, in favor of solutionary thinking.

What Is Solutionary Thinking?

Solutionary thinking consists of many forms of thinking, all of which take practice and honing. The primary components of solutionary thinking are critical thinking, systems thinking, strategic thinking, and creative thinking. While these forms of thinking are not sequential, they do build upon one another. Without critical thinking as the foundation, we cannot evaluate and understand systems clearly. Without systems think-ing, we cannot determine the best strategies for creating positive changes and act effectively. And without the first three working together, our cre-ativity may not lead to the best solutions.

Critical thinking

Like everyone, I have opinions about all sorts of things based on my worldview, beliefs, and the information I gather, and occasionally I'll catch myself expressing an impassioned statement and realize I haven't done enough research to validate its accuracy. I haven't collected credible evidence or sought out divergent viewpoints. Much to my dismay, I even made two statements in my first TEDx talk that were untrue.

Prior to giving that TEDx talk, I had learned that Uzbekistan relied upon enslaved people, often children, to work in their cotton fields and that the country produced one third of the world's cotton crop. However, I hadn't fact-checked this statistic before stating it on stage. It turns out that the actual percentage was much lower (more like 4–5% of global cotton production at the time). I also referred to the Open to Debate (formerly Intelligence Squared) topic about whether the United States was responsible for Mexico's drug war, which I discussed in chapter 1, sharing what it turns out was an entirely misheard word from the radio. Instead of saying drug *war*, I said drug *woes*. For all posterity, that talk has two errors because I failed to fact-check a statistic and a memory.[40]

What about you? Do you ever notice that you're treating statements as facts even if you don't know for certain that they are true? Do you ever share information that you think is accurate, only later to discover you misheard or misremembered? Do you, like me, often fail to corroborate information?

Most of us aren't scientists and don't do basic research. Nor are we historians who have carefully reviewed primary sources in their original languages. We rely on others whom we trust rather than on applying the scientific method, becoming experts, or going "into the field" ourselves.

It is likely that we've all stated as "fact" plenty of things that haven't been verified. Perhaps we've shared an article from a source that's not known for objectivity or thorough fact-checking, or information we saw on social media or heard from a friend. Maybe we've repeated a statistic with no citation, or a cherry-picked study that has been challenged by new or better research, or a health claim that hasn't been evaluated using double-blind methods to ascertain its validity.

How can we do due diligence before making statements and spreading potentially fallacious or misleading information? How can we stop ourselves before we present our opinions and beliefs as facts? How can we become good enough critical thinkers that we resist the desire to believe and share until after we have ensured accuracy? We can start with a commitment to be assiduous in our efforts to obtain accurate information. We can learn how to check citations, review primary sources, use reputable fact-checking sites, and analyze statistics and data carefully.

Leading up to the 2016 US presidential election, I had conversations with a number of people who were Trump supporters. One friend of mine liked Donald Trump because he shared his concerns about illegal immigration across the border with Mexico. One day he said to me that if Mexico could have a wall on its southern border, why shouldn't we be able to have a wall on our southern border.

"Mexico has a wall on its border with Guatemala?" I asked, because I'd never heard about such a wall. He assured me that it did.

When I got home, it did not take long to find images of this wall. They were all over the Internet. One was of a huge wall through a desert, under which were these words:

> This is the Border Fence Mexico built on their border with Guatemala to keep out the freeloaders. Notice The Barbed Wire & Towers with Armed Guards. Shouldn't the United States have the same right as Mexico to protect its border?

Another had a giant wall with a road on one side, which also ran through a desert, with these words superimposed on the image:

> This is the gigantic WALL that Mexico built on the Guatemalan border. Hummmm. Imagine that? I guess it is not racist for Mexico to build a wall to keep Guatemalans out.

The fact-checking site Snopes revealed that the wall accompanying the text in the first image was along Israel's border with Egypt and the wall in the text accompanying the second image was built by the United States along its border with Mexico.[41] What should have tipped off any viewer with knowledge about geography was the desert landscape in both images. The border between Mexico and Guatemala is mostly a jungle. There is no desert.

When I mentioned this to my friend, he seemed momentarily chagrined that he'd believed and shared a false statement simply because it reinforced his political beliefs, but this awareness does not seem to have made him suspicious of other statements from the media that support his worldview. Like most of us, he believes that his sources are providing facts and sharing information accurately.

It's hard to resist believing (and sharing) what we're told by the pundits, influencers, leaders, family members, friends, and others whom we respect and admire. It's also hard to believe information we don't want to believe, especially if it comes from those whom we consider "other," even if that information is accurate. As the late journalist Sydney J. Harris wrote, "We believe what we want to believe, what we like to believe, what suits our prejudices and fuels our passions."[42]

It seems our species is innately skilled at confirmation bias, the tendency to interpret or selectively seek out information in ways that support our existing beliefs and to disregard or downplay contrary evidence. To be a solutionary, however, it's important not only to be vigilant about fact-checking and thinking critically about information presented as "fact" but also to not automatically dismiss information just because it comes from a source or group we have previously put into the category of "them."

What qualities support good critical thinking? The following list is an adaptation from the work of Dr. Linda Elder and Dr. Richard Paul, who have written extensively on the "critical thinking mindset."[43] Some of the attitudes of good critical thinkers that they cite include:

- open-mindedness,
- healthy skepticism,
- intellectual humility,
- awareness of personal and cultural biases, and
- motivation to put in the time to think critically.

To help you put in the time to think critically and practice your critical thinking skills, I recommend Professor Wayne Bartz's CRITIC method. CRITIC is an acronym that stands for:

- **Claim?**
- **Role of claimant?**
- **Information backing the claim?**

- **T**est?
- **Independent testing?**
- **Cause proposed?**

You can use the questions from this acronym to analyze any claim. For example, imagine that it's 2021 and you saw a Facebook post from a doctor claiming that the COVID vaccines are dangerous and you shouldn't get them. Instead, he argues, you should take a supplement that will protect you against COVID. The post offers examples of people who got the vaccine and had adverse reactions and provides a link to his website where you can order the supplement.

How would you use the CRITIC method to evaluate the claim?

1. What is the claim?
   The COVID vaccine is dangerous, changes people's genetics, and doesn't work. A supplement will protect you from COVID.
2. What is the role of the claimant?
   He is an osteopathic doctor who sells the supplement and is opposed to vaccines.
3. What information backs up the claim?
   There are anecdotal stories about people who had adverse reactions to the COVID vaccine and a link to a non-peer-reviewed study that mentions the chemical in the supplement.
4. Was any test to prove the claim conducted?
   There is no evidence of a test.
5. Was any independent testing conducted?
   There's no information about this in the post.
6. What is the cause proposed for the claim?
   The proposed cause for the danger of the vaccines is that they change a person's genetics. There is no proposed cause for the effectiveness of the supplement.

I've based the above example on a real Facebook post—since removed because of persistent falsehoods—from a controversial osteopathic doctor who has been making tens of millions of dollars on his unproven supplements as he simultaneously critiques—without evidence—the science that has led to vaccines against and treatments for COVID.

Try the CRITIC method and notice the impact of the process on your thinking, perspectives, and emotions. In particular, try using it to analyze a claim you believe but have not validated. You may discover some cognitive dissonance whereby your deeply held belief begins to conflict with new information. You may also discover that you're developing better critical thinking skills, greater nuance, a bit more skepticism, and increasing curiosity.

All of us can be manipulated by misinformation and disinformation, especially if it comes from a respected source like a doctor and/or reinforces our fears and beliefs. When I visited classrooms as a humane educator in the 1990s, I'd often put on a white lab coat during my presentation and ask the students what assumptions or judgments they had about me because of the article of clothing I'd just put on. They would usually say that the lab coat made them feel I was more trustworthy, smarter, and that I cared about them. A cheap lab coat—something that can be purchased for less than $20—packs a wallop of assumptions. (I also told my students not to believe a word I said and to be prepared to validate my statements for themselves.)

So when a doctor wearing a lab coat in a photo on his Facebook post secures our subconscious trust with his garment, tells us that the COVID vaccine is dangerous and his supplements are safe, shares stories of people who've had bad reactions to the vaccine, and points to a study that says a supplement is effective at preventing COVID—it's not unlikely that our amygdala (the part of our brain that detects danger and initiates a fight or flight response) reacts to the threat he presented with fear and the offer of the supplement with relief. It should not be surprising that so many people are inclined to believe him (why would he lie?), to share the information (because they care about others), and to buy the supplement (because their health is at stake and they are hedging their bets). For those people who are already suspicious of and/or opposed to vaccines, the post would also reinforce their fears.

Instead of believing the claim, however, the CRITIC method asks us to step back just long enough to engage our critical thinking. The method requires that we use our prefrontal cortex (the part of our brain that regulates our thoughts, actions, and emotions) so that our immediate reactions do not have the last word in terms of our actions. With practice, the CRITIC method can become second nature, and our critical thinking skills will get better and better.

To hone our critical thinking skills, it's also helpful to ask ourselves the following, some of which are variations on the CRITIC questions:

- Where does the information come from? Is it a reliable source? How do I know?
- Is the information a verifiable fact? An opinion? Propaganda?
- Is the information supported by credible evidence? Can I access that evidence myself?
- Has the information been peer reviewed?[44]
- What are the author's/speaker's credentials or organizational affiliations? Is the author/speaker qualified to write/speak on the topic?

Next, to evaluate bias, we can ask:

- What is the purpose of the information? Is there an agenda or conflict of interest?
- Do the authors/speakers/sponsors make their intentions or purpose clear?
- If the information includes a study, who funded the study?
- Are there political, ideological, cultural, religious, economic, institutional, or personal views expressed or assumed?
- What are my own biases in regard to the information?

Systems thinking

We are composed of systems and live amidst systems. Like other animals, we have a circulatory system, nervous system, digestive system, reproductive system, and so on. We are also inextricably connected to and live within ecosystems, such as soil systems, water systems, weather systems, et cetera.

When I use the term "systems" in the context of systems thinking, I'm referring not only to biological and ecological systems but also to human-created systems: structures, procedures, and networks that consist of interrelated and interdependent elements, such as economic systems, legal systems, energy systems, defense systems, food systems, media systems, political systems, et cetera.

Systems thinking requires a commitment to examine highly complex, interconnected societal and ecological systems. While we don't need to become experts in these systems, we do need to be able to identify and understand the connections between them. It would, in fact, be impossible to become an expert in more than a couple of systems. Think of scientists you know or have heard of, and you'll quickly notice that they are experts in a fairly narrow field of study within a specific scientific discipline. They are not astrophysicists, marine biologists, mycologists, virologists, and ethologists at the same time.

The same is true for experts in social systems. Some are knowledgeable about economics, or law, or transportation, or education. Only the very rare person will be deeply knowledgeable about many systems. But it is eminently possible to recognize the interplay between societal systems and feel empowered and motivated to learn from people with experience in different fields to gain perspective and knowledge about the impacts of solutions in a range of systems. Moreover, we must strive to do so because solutions can have unintended negative consequences if we do not consider their *systemic* impacts.

One of the primary jobs of a solutionary is to identify the flaws, problems, and the unintended negative consequences within societal systems; recognize the many factors that lead to their creation and adoption, and seek to transform them and/or develop new, more sustainable and equitable systems. By doing this, solutionaries pave the way for those who might not be inclined to "buck the system" through making out-of-the-mainstream personal choices, as well as those without the means to do so, to participate in the newly developed and healthier systems.

Not only can and do people transform systems, systems can and do transform us. Consider the myriad systems that have arisen in the past one hundred and fifty years (e.g., telephone communications, electrified buildings, internal combustion engines, air travel, plastic production, personal computers, the Internet, cell phones, smart phones, GPS navigation, social media, artificial intelligence chatbots, etc.). Societies have changed because of these systems, and people's beliefs and behaviors have shifted in response.

Sometimes new systems are profoundly helpful, dramatically improving our quality of life. Sometimes they are helpful but also have serious negative impacts. Sometimes we are barely aware when pernicious new systems that are cruel and destructive arise and gain traction.

I believe we can and will become more morally aware and consistently ethical, and transforming systems will be one of the biggest contributors to this shift. Once our lives are embedded within healthier and more humane systems, we will likely look back on many of our current systems with shock and dismay, the way we look back on other times in history when we perpetrated cruelty, injustice, and destruction as the norm. We will become more ethical through the development of more ethical systems. But to transform systems, we need to become competent systems thinkers.

At the Institute for Humane Education, we developed an activity called True Price to help people practice both critical and systems thinking.[45] Through the activity's questions, people improve their investigative and thinking skills. Here's a brief overview of the activity:

TRUE PRICE

Choose an item to examine. It could be a food or beverage, an electronic device, an article of clothing, a personal care product—anything at all. Then ask yourself the following questions about it:

1. What are the positive and negative effects, through production, use, and disposal, of this item on:

   - me?
   - other people?

- animals?
- the environment?

2. What systems make this item easy to acquire and ubiquitous?

3. Are there alternatives that do more good and less harm, and, if so, what systems would need to change to make such alternatives affordable, easily accessible, and commonplace?

4. If no such alternatives exist, what systems would need to change to make alternatives more likely to be developed?

Chances are that the item you examine—assuming you choose a purchased item as opposed to an item like a cherry you picked off a tree—will have tentacles that reach across the globe and will be connected to the systems of energy; transportation; ecology; production; agriculture, logging, and/or mining; waste disposal; economics; politics; media and advertising; infrastructure, and more.

Almost twenty years ago, driving home after a long hike, Edwin and I stopped to get gas. I had finished drinking the water I'd brought with me that day and was thirsty, so I went into the gas station's convenience store to buy a bottle of water. Choosing among the brands, I found myself drawn to one I'd never seen before. It was called Fiji, and it was in a square bottle with a pretty pink flower on the label. It evoked beauty, adventure, and a tropical paradise. I came back to the car with the bottle, and Edwin asked to look at it. After reading the label, he said, "I can't believe you bought this."

True, it was uncommon for me to buy bottled beverages, especially water. After all, I could have refilled my reusable water bottle in the convenience store's bathroom, and we both knew that buying single-use beverages didn't align with my values.

Still, I was surprised by his comment, and so I responded, "What do you mean?"

"This water comes from Fiji."

"No way!" I replied. "It's just *called* Fiji water." I couldn't imagine that it had truly been transported from a Pacific island on the other side of the world.

My husband read the label to me, which clearly stated its Fijian origins. I responded with what was the only silver lining I could think of to my unMOGO choice. I told him I would use that bottle for the rest of my life to illustrate the True Price activity. And that's what I've been doing ever since.

The more research I conducted on bottled water in general—and Fiji in particular—the more waste and pollution was revealed.[46] Not only does bottling water use fossil fuels for both plastic production and the transportation and refrigeration of the bottles, but the process wastes water itself. It can take several liters of water to produce a single liter of bottled water! Moreover, I also learned that a significant percentage of Fijians don't have access to clean water, even as an aquifer in their country is being pumped by a foreign corporation for its own profits.[47]

The deeper we dig as we delve into True Price, the more we will discover, and the more questions we will find ourselves asking and seeking to answer. Through web searches, we'll have the ability to gain knowledge that was almost impossible to find before the age of the Internet. Of course, we'll have to be careful, because we will likely find misinformation and/or disinformation too, perhaps even from the company website whose item we're analyzing.

Although this research takes effort, you will likely find it fascinating (albeit potentially disturbing). And while you may wish to embrace quick and simple answers to the problems that you discover through your research, the key to being a solutionary is a willingness to dig ever more deeply.

For example, let's say that you learn that a clothing brand you like outsources its production to overseas factories over which it has no control. Further, you learn that these factories mistreat employees. You no longer want to support the company so you decide to boycott the brand. Does this help solve the problem?

Unless you also engage in an effort to change the policies at the clothing company and/or in the overseas factory, or the laws that govern what corporations in your country are allowed to do in relation to utilizing over-seas companies that violate your own country's human rights laws, you're not actually helping the people working in that factory. The reason they are working under abysmal conditions is because those jobs are better than their alternatives. To really help them, you'll need to consider the systems that perpetuate such mistreatment and find places to intervene to change those systems while simultaneously choosing clothing that supports companies that are more aligned with your values and then letting the company that you're boycotting know why you aren't buying their clothing any more.

How can you change such systems? The answer to that question brings us to strategic thinking.

Strategic thinking

Strategic thinking builds upon everything else you've read up to now. As you gain practice cultivating a solutionary mindset and lens, hone your critical thinking, and uncover systems, you'll begin to see which systems need to change, but you may feel confounded by the complexities of sys-tem-intersections that stymie those changes.

It's time to think strategically.

Thinking strategically means identifying leverage points for change and determining how you might intervene successfully at those points. Just as a lever enables someone to lift a weight that would otherwise be difficult to budge, a leverage point is a place where a small force can have a big impact. Finding and using levers for change leads to powerful transformations in systems and is personally exciting and empowering.

As an example of strategic thinking, consider the Delancey Street Foundation, a nonprofit organization addressing the problems of recidivism among criminals, relapse among people addicted to drugs, and violence between rival gang members. Given that there are so many obstacles for ex-convicts to reintegrate into society, for people suffering from addiction and alcoholism to become permanently sober, and for bridge-building between gang members, what strategies could work? With few job op-portunities and a lack of support and accountability for ex-convicts and those with addictions, little affordable housing, and pervasive violence

among rival gangs, how could Delancey Street possibly fir
points for so many intersecting obstacles?

Their answer was to leverage several systems in a synergistic way to
have the greatest chance of overall success. Delancey Street Foundation
created an educational residential self-help and jobs program to provide
housing, support, education, and employment for its residents, who
range in age from eighteen to sixty-eight and include men and women of
all races and ethnicities, mostly unskilled, functionally illiterate, and with
a personal history of violence and generational poverty. These residents
live together for a minimum of two years. They work toward and receive
their high school equivalency degree (GED) and are trained in three different marketable skills. Using a system they call "each one teach one,"
every new resident is responsible for helping guide the next arrival.[48]

Delancey Street Foundation has built many thriving businesses, from
accounting to construction to landscaping, that employ their current
and former residents, and they have duplicated their model in several cities. As of this writing, they've successfully reintegrated more than
20,000 people into society. These graduates of Delancey Street are now
able to support themselves, stay sober, and stay out of prison. It's a powerful strategic approach to several challenging and systemic problems in
our society.

If the Delancey Street Foundation can solve such seemingly intractable and complex problems, we can surely solve narrower problems within
our own spheres of influence. In chapter 5, you'll have the opportunity
to think strategically and explore leverage points to solve a problem you
care about, one that is both meaningful and feasible for you.

Creative thinking

Why does creative thinking come last? Wouldn't it make more sense to
cultivate one's creative thinking right off the bat? Isn't the capacity to
ideate and manipulate thoughts in novel ways going to generate good
ideas from the get-go? Perhaps. And I'm not suggesting you save creative
thinking until after you've thought critically, systemically, and strategically. In fact, creativity will likely have been helping and guiding you all
along. However, if you want to be a solutionary, your creative thinking

around a problem you want to solve needs to be grounded in critical thinking, systems thinking, and strategic thinking.

How will you cultivate creative thinking after laying this groundwork? There are many creative ways! After learning about a problem, doing research to understand the systems that perpetuate it, and considering the leverage points for change, you might:

- Take a long walk and allow your mind to relax and be open.
- Convene a group to brainstorm ideas with you, choosing people who care about the problem but come with expertise in different fields and arenas. The brainstorm is likely to get your own creative thinking flowing.
- Incubate a dream by asking yourself a question about the problem over and over in your head before going to sleep.
- Write a poem, draw a picture, compose a song, make a sculpture, choreograph a dance, draft the outline of a play—any kind of artistic outlet that allows you to work through the issues you've learned about in an imaginative way. What reveals itself through art may lead to innovative ideas for solving the problem(s) you care about.

———

You may find that your brain gets tired with all this thinking, just like your body gets tired after a workout. But just as a hard workout leaves you feeling exhausted but full of happiness-enhancing endorphins (not to mention a healthier body), a good brain workout leaves you feeling tired but mentally enriched, engaged, and enthused.

Challenge the Ten Instincts

The late Hans Rosling, a Swedish physician, founder of Gapminder,[49] a nonprofit fighting global misconceptions, and the author of *Factfulness: Ten Reasons We're Wrong About the World—And Why Things Are Better Than You Think,* offers the following ten instincts to pay attention to and temper. Challenging these instincts is very useful for people who want to develop their solutionary thinking skills.

As you read through this list, compiled by Sam Thomas Davies on his website,[50] notice and consider the many times you have experienced these instincts:

- **The Gap Instinct.** Our tendency to divide things into two distinct and often conflicting groups with an imagined gap between them (e.g., us versus them).
- **The Negativity Instinct.** Our tendency to notice the bad more than the good (e.g., believing that things are getting worse when things may actually be getting better).
- **The Straight Line Instinct.** Our tendency to assume that a statistical trend will continue in a straight line, even though such lines are rare in reality.
- **The Fear Instinct.** Our hardwired tendency to pay more attention to frightening things.
- **The Size Instinct.** Our tendency to get things out of proportion, or misjudge the size of things.
- **The Generalization Instinct.** Our tendency to mistakenly group together things, people, or countries that are actually very different.
- **The Destiny Instinct.** The idea that innate characteristics determine the destinies of people, countries, religions, or cultures, that things are as they are because of inescapable reasons.
- **The Single Perspective Instinct.** Our tendency to focus on a single cause or perspective when it comes to understanding the world (e.g., forming our worldview by relying on the media we consume alone).
- **The Blame Instinct.** Our tendency to find one clear, simple reason for why something bad has happened.
- **The Urgency Instinct.** Our tendency to take immediate action in the face of perceived imminent danger, and in doing so, amplify our other instincts.

If these are instincts we want to watch out for, a solutionary instinct is one we want to cultivate.

Chapter 4:

PREPARING FOR YOUR
SOLUTIONARY PRACTICE

The Institute for Humane Education (IHE) has developed a Solutionary Framework, a four-phase process that teaches people how to be solutionaries. Educators across six continents and in most states in the United States are using this framework with their students. Some are integrating it into their existing curricula. Some are using it alongside lessons about the UN Sustainable Development Goals (SDGs) so their students can develop solutions to help achieve these goals.[51] Some have made it a stand-alone elective course. Some use it in afterschool programs. And some schools are infusing the framework into their entire school.

At IHE, we began our solutionary work focusing on schools because we believe that education is the system that lies at the root of all other societal systems. I wrote a book, *The World Becomes What We Teach: Educating a Generation of Solutionaries,* to share why and how to infuse the Solutionary Framework into the education system. This approach remains my primary strategy for changing a core system to help build a world where other systems become healthier and more equitable.

The reason I've written this book is to introduce *everyone* to the solutionary process so that any reader, regardless of their profession and sphere of influence, can identify the system(s) they wish to change. So what will your strategy be? What issue or issues will you seek to address? This chapter invites you to begin to imagine the answers to these questions, so that you will be ready to embark on the four-phase solutionary process in chapter 5.

What can you expect personally from the solutionary process? To summarize some of what I've already written, these are some likely outcomes:

• deeper compassion and understanding

- more connections to people who inspire you
- greater meaning and purpose
- increased self-respect coupled with humility
- a stronger sense of agency and efficacy

It's also likely that you'll find yourself recovering from some or all of the following:

- either/or and us-versus-them thinking
- siloed media exposure and polarization
- apathy
- isolation
- hopelessness

I say this with some confidence because I have seen the positive impacts of the solutionary process on the graduate students who go through our doctoral and master's programs, on the teachers who implement the Solutionary Framework in their classrooms, and on the young people who learn how to become solutionaries and describe the process as the best part of their education.[52] They reinforce what singer-songwriter Joan Baez once said: "Action is the antidote to despair."[53] It is their enthusiastic responses to the solutionary approach that lead me to believe that it can transform not only destructive and inhumane systems but also, as I've already mentioned, the lives of the solutionaries themselves.

What Is the Story and Path That Led You to This Process?

Before diving into the solutionary process, it's worthwhile to take some time to reflect upon your personal history up to this point. What issues and problems have most concerned you in your life? What's your change-making story thus far? Do you have such a story?

Here's mine: I did not grow up perceiving myself as a potential change-maker (let alone a solutionary). I didn't know such people and hadn't been raised by my parents or taught in school to believe that I could or should try to change destructive and oppressive systems. Growing up in the 1960s and 70s, I'd seen Vietnam War protesters on TV, but outside of that kind of activism, I didn't have a sense of what it would mean to work for change. I saw myself as a person who would pursue a career, and to the degree that I would change anything for the better, I supposed it would be through a chosen profession.

Growing up during the second wave of the feminist movement, I entertained many potential professions. One of them was astronaut, an unusual career goal for a girl in the 1970s, but after I'd discovered *Star Trek* at age thirteen and had become an obsessive fan, I longed to explore space like the crew of the starship *Enterprise*, so astronaut seemed like a logical career choice. (Logical decisions became important to me per Mr. Spock's modeling, and yes, I did realize that *Star Trek* was fictional, but I hoped it was prophetic.) At fourteen I started working at a *Star Trek* store in Manhattan, which reinforced my extraterrestrial goals, and a year later I even asked William Shatner, who played Captain Kirk on the original *Star Trek* series, to kiss me in front of five thousand people at a *Star Trek* convention. Granted, this was not a route toward space travel, let alone toward a solutionary career, but perhaps my bold request was prescient of a willingness to do what it takes to achieve my goals, which is probably the most generous interpretation of my choice to publicly humiliate myself as a teenager.[54]

Although I remain a *Star Trek* fan to this day, and the *Star Trek* vision of a future in which we've solved so many of our challenges is still a beacon for me, by the time I went to college, I'd settled on becoming a physician rather than an astronaut. Quickly, though, I realized that I wasn't ready for the slog that is premed, so I put that career path on what would become a permanent hold and became an English major, graduating with both a bachelor's and master's degree and entertaining the idea of getting a Ph.D. and becoming a college professor. But the job market for English professors was dismal, and I wanted a bit more job security. When a close friend was applying to law school and I was floundering and without direction, I applied, too. I lasted three months in law school before realizing that law was the wrong profession for me. Two years later I went to Divinity School to pursue a master's degree in Theological Studies studying comparative religion, job security be damned.

ettante (many did), but the truth was that I hadn't yet
..t I could turn what I cared about into my life's work, so
: time to find my way. What *did* I care about other than
...n high school and early college, I was passionate about racial
jus... .y the end of college, I'd added women's rights and environ-
mentalism to my concerns. I had always adored animals, and as a child
longed to be like Jane Goodall,[55] but I wasn't sure how to embark on that
path so I'd abandoned that dream before even trying. Then I read Peter
Singer's book *Animal Liberation* and learned about the many forms of
institutionalized cruelty to animals. I was stunned by the hidden animal
suffering that permeated virtually every aspect of my life, from what I
ate, to what I wore, to the shampoo I used. Animal abuse soon became
my focus.

Eventually, I found a way to combine all the issues I cared about into a
career as a comprehensive humane educator, but during those years when I
focused primarily on animal rights, some people criticized me for caring
more about animals than people. In fact, a therapist I saw in my mid-twen-
ties pathologized my desire to work on behalf of animals, urging me to
reflect upon what she clearly considered to be a combination of an emotional problem and a character flaw.

So that's a bit of my story, and part of the reason I am telling you about
it is to drive home the importance of identifying and embracing what *you*
really care about and staying open to finding *your* particular path. The
world is full of problems. There is so much suffering to be found. If we
each focus on what matters most to us while making sure to minimize
any negative impacts of our solutions on people, animals, and the environment, we will collectively contribute to a world with fewer problems
and less suffering.

What Are You Good At? What Do You Love to Do?

While you're learning about and practicing the solutionary process in the
next chapter, keep these two questions in mind:

- What am I good at?
- What do I love to do?

When you find the place where the answers to these two questions meet and then direct them toward what you care about, you will likely find yourself on a path to a deeply rewarding life of growth, purpose, and contribution. While none of us know all the answers to these questions, and presumably we will continually discover new things we're good at and love to do, most of us have some immediate responses.

As you think about what you're good at, consider those things that aren't generally measured, but which are important nonetheless. Do you make friends easily? Are you able to lead projects? Are you tech savvy? Can you organize events? Are you a skilled researcher and fact-finder? Are you comfortable with public speaking? Are you artistic, musical, or creative in some other way? Do you make people laugh? Are you a good listener? Are you persuasive? Are you handy and able to build and create things?

Any of these qualities and skills can be directed toward your solutionary efforts and help you to succeed in solving the problems you care about. If you choose those activities and approaches that you also enjoy doing, then you'll be continually rewarded and motivated to persist in your efforts. Another win-win.

During my circuitous journey toward a career as a humane educator, I discovered I was good at teaching and writing, and I loved doing both. Applying these skills to the issues I cared about was my win-win.

Did You Know?

To whet your appetite for the solutionary process, I offer this "Did you know?" section, meant to spur you to ask yourself questions as you pay close attention to what's happening around you, and to notice what lies below the surface on billboards and in boardrooms, in supermarkets and stock markets, in your local ecology and your nation's psychology.

Did you know...
that an organic apple sometimes costs the same amount of money as a fast-food burger?

At the Institute for Humane Education's campus in Maine, there are dozens of apple trees. They have sprouted up as "volunteers" from six old trees, one of which was planted around 1900. This very old tree still produces abundant and delicious apples. No work is required on our part except very occasional pruning.

The trees on our property produce so many apples that we cannot possibly eat and preserve them all. Nor can we give them all away (we've tried). Nor do the deer and porcupines eat them all. Many of them rot on the trees over the winter.

Given that this is just one tiny example of the abundance of organic apples across the United States, isn't it odd that organic apples sometimes cost more than $1.50 each, equivalent to a cheap fast-food burger.[56]

Consider what is involved in producing a fast-food burger:

- Feed crops are grown, irrigated, sprayed with pesticides and fertilizers, harvested, and transported to feedlots where cows are fattened prior to slaughter.
- A cow is raised, fed, watered, has her waste removed, is transported to a meatpacking facility, slaughtered, disemboweled, cut up and ground up, formed into patties, transported on refrigerated trucks, and kept refrigerated or frozen until purchase.
- Wheat is grown, irrigated, sprayed with pesticides and fertilizers, harvested, processed into flour, baked into a bun, and transported.
- Tomatoes, lettuce, onions, and cucumbers are planted, fertilized, sprayed with pesticides, harvested, transported, kept refrigerated, pickled (in the case of the cucumbers), and sliced.
- Condiments that are processed in factories using a variety of ingredients are grown, harvested, and/or procured from animals (e.g., the eggs in mayonnaise) before being packaged in plastic and/or aluminum.
- Someone cooks the burger and puts all these ingredients together.
- The burgers are packaged for sale.
- Companies market and advertise their burgers to compete with other fast-food chains.

With all that goes into a fast-food burger, does it make any sense that it can cost about the same amount as an organic apple? How is this even possible?

It's only possible because of taxpayer subsidies.[57] In the United States, taxpayers fund the meat and dairy industries through subsidies that amount to an estimated $38 billion annually.[58] According to Christopher Bellmann, globally "between 2015 and 2017 more than $620 billion was paid in annual transfers to the agricultural sector by the twenty largest-producing countries for which subsidy data are available."[59] These massive sums do not include the taxpayer subsidies that are spent on healthcare to combat the preventable illnesses caused by eating excessive amounts of fast food, nor the subsidies for cleaning up the environment from the destructive impacts on soil, water, and air. In other words, the health impacts, climate change impacts, biodiversity loss impacts, soil erosion impacts, and pollution impacts all add up to a significant amount, too, even though they are not factored into the actual price the consumer pays.[60] In contrast, the negative impacts of organic apples are minimal.

Did you know...
that while slavery is illegal everywhere, there are thirty-five to forty-five million enslaved people in the world, with more than 400,000 in the United States?

According to the NGO Anti-Slavery, slavery today takes many forms, including human trafficking, forced labor, debt bondage, child slavery, sex trafficking, and forced marriage.[61]

While slavery is universally condemned and illegal, it persists largely because of poverty, which leads many to fall prey to traps and exploitation. Desperation leads parents to relinquish their children, often believing manipulative and dishonest traffickers who convince them that their children will prosper under their care.

Enslaved children and adults are working in cotton fields and on cocoa farms. They are tying knots in handwoven rugs, dismantling electronics in the e-waste industry, and mining gold. The chocolate you eat, cotton T-shirt you buy, and gold ring you purchase may be tainted by slavery without you ever knowing.

Did you know...
that the 1944 GI Bill, which provided low-cost mortgages,
low-interest loans to start a business or farm,
and free education to all American veterans,
led to greater racial wealth disparities?

The GI Bill, also known as the Servicemen's Readjustment Act of 1944, was a law passed by the US Congress that provided a range of benefits to American military veterans returning from World War II. It was designed to help veterans by providing financial assistance for education, home loans, and job training, and it increased access to higher education and home ownership for millions of Americans.

While the GI Bill was colorblind in theory, in practice it accommodated Jim Crow laws. If you were African American and weren't permitted to attend college or buy a home due to discrimination, the theoretical benefits of the GI Bill were of little value in practice. In fact, because the GI Bill enabled all white veterans to gain education and accumulate wealth in the postwar years, but only a small portion of African American veterans, it drove even greater racial gaps in wealth and education over time.[62]

To this day, these inequities not only persist but continue to grow, driven by long-standing systems that impact where people live and their access to good schools and job opportunities.[63]

Did you know...
that the consolidation of food systems has led to monopolies
and feedback loops that can threaten food security?

Just a few corporations account for the vast majority of seeds, farm machinery, agro-chemicals, and market share of corn, wheat, rice, and soybeans—the primary crops currently grown for human consumption, animal feed, and biofuels. These companies' vast market share has led to their political power through lobbying. By one estimate, four companies control 90% of global grain trade.[64] Through mergers and vertical consolidation, they are able to sell seeds that are genetically engineered to be grown with the herbicides that they also manufacture.

While it may seem like varieties of food are abundant, in reality there has been a genetic narrowing. According to the United Nations, the world's crops have lost 75% of their genetic diversity since 1900.[65] This diversity loss increases the danger of diseases, fungal infections, and pathogens impacting current crops. With growing resistance to herbicides, superweeds also become threats. With fewer varieties to resist droughts and floods, climate change then becomes an ever-greater risk to food security.

Is your mind whirring? Then it's time to dive into the solutionary process. The solutionary mindset, MOGO principle, solutionary thinking, and solutionary preparation that you have been exploring thus far in this book have prepared you to take the next step and begin what I like to think of as a "solutionary practice." Just as we may practice a musical instrument or have a meditation practice, so too do we practice being a solutionary. Before you begin this practice, however, here's one more suggestion to consider.

Strive to Be a Campfire Rather Than a Forest Fire

There's a metaphor I like to use when talking to people who aspire to be solutionaries. I ask them to imagine two fires. The first is a campfire. The fire is warm and bright, and people are drawn toward it. Their faces glow in the firelight, and there is nowhere they'd rather be.

Now picture too much fuel added to this fire. Sparks begin to fly upward and ignite a tree. The flames quickly spread, and what was a campfire turns into a forest fire. It becomes difficult to breathe, and everyone flees, desperate to escape.

What can we learn from these two fires?

We each have a fire inside of us. It is the fire of our passions, and those of us who are driven to be solutionaries know it well. It is the fire that spurs us to learn about what is happening on our planet—to people, animals, and the environment—and it is the fire that motivates us to challenge and address the atrocities that still exist in our world. Sometimes our fire is blazing hot. Other times, if we've burned out, it is a barely glowing ember. There is a reason for the word "burnout" after all.

As solutionaries, we have a choice about what sort of fire we will strive to be. Hopefully, we will seek to be a warm, welcoming campfire that draws people toward us so that we can share what we know, inspire others to make a difference, and build a community to help solve our collective problems. It's possible, though, that we will succumb to our anger and become more like the forest fire that rages too hot, causing people to run from us.

How you tend your fire makes an enormous difference in your effectiveness as a solutionary. Because fire is not static, whichever fire you have been, or are today, is subject to change. Much depends on the fuel. Fires die out if we don't add fuel. At the same time, too much fuel added too quickly can ignite an inferno. We know that our fire needs more fuel if we aren't contributing in meaningful ways to positive change. We also know that we need to limit our fuel to control our fire if people start avoiding us because we're burning too hot and too angrily.

The fuel I'm referring to is information about suffering, injustice, and destruction. As inquiry becomes a default mindset, we will continually become aware of problems. This "information fuel" can sometimes overwhelm our ability to maintain equanimity, remain nonjudgmental of others, and manage our anger in a healthy way by directing it positively toward solutionary actions. If we have added too much fuel and are noticing its negative effects, we may need to step back, spend more time with loved ones, enjoy the outdoors, participate in creative pursuits, and limit our exposure to information about problems. While we cannot just choose to avoid or limit information about problems that impact us immediately and directly, if the problems we're learning about are further removed, and if we are falling into despair through overexposure, stepping back from endless bad news may be important to avoid burnout. The reverse can sometimes become a problem, too. If we don't actively practice inquiry, we won't have the "information fuel" to drive our solutionary efforts. Again, just as a fire needs tending through providing the right amount of fuel, so do we.

I share this advice from experience. I know that despite my best intentions, there are times I still burn too hot. Sometimes I fail to communicate thoughtfully and am too aggressive in my speech and actions, consumed as I am by my own rage about the harms we cause and my frustration when others aren't concerned. I've learned to temper my sometimes fiery nature by moderating my exposure to atrocities and balancing the seemingly endless fuel of bad news with time in the natural world, meditation, daily exercise, walks with our dogs, and reminding myself that things can be bad and better at the same time. Most of the time, I'm able to find balance, but not always. I know the frustration that can build when others don't "get it," when changes I perceive as obvious and clear seem elusive even after decades of work, when I see setbacks instead of advances, when people around me knowingly make lifestyle choices that perpetuate injustice, animal cruelty, and environmental destruction and do not seem to care. I know that I should hold my tongue lest people run from my occasional outbursts, but sometimes I fail to wisely respond and instead quickly react.

There's a well-known Aesop fable about the sun and the wind. The wind challenges the sun to a contest to see who can get a person walking on the ground below to take off their coat. The wind goes first. It blows as hard as it can, trying to force the coat off, but the person simply wraps the coat more tightly around their body until the wind is exhausted. When it's the sun's turn, it shines as brightly as possible. Soon the person is wiping their brow and removing their coat. The sun—that fireball the perfect distance from Earth—burned just right.

As you embark on your solutionary practice, you'll want to burn just right, too.

Chapter 5:

THE FOUR PHASES OF THE
SOLUTIONARY PROCESS

T HE SOLUTIONARY PROCESS is divided into four phases, each of which has three steps. This process guides people through identifying a problem they wish to solve, researching it thoroughly, developing solutions, and choosing and implementing a solution. This chapter will describe and illustrate these phases so that you can embark on your own solutionary practice.

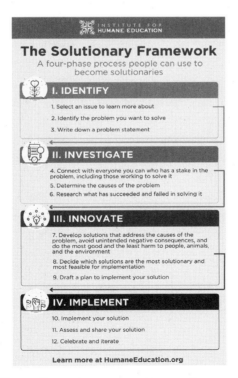

Fig 5.1: CREDIT: INSTITUTE FOR HUMANE EDUCATION

Phase I: Identify

1. Select an issue to learn more about
2. Identify the problem you want to solve
3. Write down a problem statement

In Phase I, Identify, you'll dive into learning all you can about an issue of concern to you and then focus on an aspect that you can successfully address given your time constraints, sphere of influence, support, and skill set. You'll complete Phase I by articulating a problem statement to guide you during the next phases of the solutionary process.

Select an issue to learn more about

You may be coming to the solutionary process with a problem that already concerns you. It could fall into the category of environmental destruction or social injustice or animal abuse. Maybe it revolves around a system that has become largely dysfunctional, such as siloed media, partisan politics, or threats to democracy. Perhaps it's an overarching issue that affects virtually everyone and everything such as climate change. Maybe the reflection you did in the previous chapter has left you with new ideas about an issue you want to explore. Perhaps you want to examine a close-to-home problem like the amount of waste you produce or living a lifestyle with a high carbon footprint. Or maybe the problem you want to solve is one that is personally harming you and your family.

Whether you come to this process unsure about a problem to address or highly focused on an issue of concern to you, consider this first phase an opportunity to simply learn. Because problems—whether in your household, neighborhood, country, or world—are connected through complex intersecting systems, exploring deeply will be important not only so that you will be able to identify a specific, solvable problem to address but also to ensure you'll be able to solve it *in a solutionary way*, doing the most good and least harm.

Below is a chart with six problems, a brief description of who and what are affected by these problems, and some of their impacts. (A longer list can be found in appendix 4.) Be aware as you read the chart that follows that I've chosen a few big challenges as examples and that this list is by no means representative of the many and varied problems in our societies and world. You may want to explore an entirely different problem unrelated to any of the following. This list is also not meant to suggest that you will be starting your solutionary journey by attempting to solve one of these large, overarching problems. Rather, it is meant to invite you to learn more so that in the next step, when you consider local manifestations of a big problem, you will have a base of knowledge from which to choose a specific issue to address.

Problem	Who/What Is Affected (People, Animals, and/or Ecosystems)	Impacts
Climate change	All	• The majority of people and nations are impacted and, to greater and lesser degrees, are perpetuating the problem. • The problem impacts myriad species and poses an existential threat to people and animals living on low-lying islands and in coastal regions as well as those without the means to move or adjust to climate impacts. • It is causing increased fires, droughts, floods, heat, storms, coral bleaching, desertification, extinctions, and is creating climate refugees.
Poverty	Affects those living in poverty and also has negative effects on society in general. Poverty can affect animals through poaching and habitat destruction.	• Poverty leads to a host of problems, including overall human suffering, homelessness, malnutrition, lack of access to clean water, ill health and lack of access to healthcare, reduced lifespan, etc. • Poverty also leads to societal dysfunction and is a sign of societal inequity—a related problem. • Those living in poverty may have no choice but to poach wildlife or destroy habitat for food and fuel.

Problem	Who/What Is Affected (People, Animals, and/or Ecosystems)	Impacts
Modern-day animal agriculture (factory farming)	All	• Factory farming practices are responsible for animal cruelty, pollution, soil erosion, ocean dead zones, antibiotic resistance, and health problems. • Factory farming is one of the biggest contributors to climate change. • Slaughterhouse work is among the most dangerous jobs with workers routinely suffering debilitating injuries.
Isms (racism, sexism, classism, ableism, etc.)	People	• These isms have become embedded in societal structures and systems (to greater and lesser degrees depending upon the society and the specific ism). While efforts to address these isms have been pursued for decades and sometimes centuries, and progress has been and continues to be made, they persist. • Additionally, isms do not operate in isolation, and they reflect inter-connected systems of oppression that can magnify the harms inflicted on groups with multiple marginalized identities. • (Speciesism, not included in this chart, is an ism that affects animals.)
Animal cruelty (not only in food production, but also trapping, hunting, poaching, fishing, animal experimentation, trafficking, poi-soning, rodeos,	Primarily animals, but also people and the environment	• While most people are opposed to animal cruelty, it persists not only in food production but also in the clothing, entertainment, sport hunting/fishing industries, in research and testing, and wildlife management industries. • Obviously animals suffer from animal cruelty, but people may as well, especially those who become

Problem	Who/What Is Affected (People, Animals, and/or Ecosystems)	Impacts
circuses, horse and dog racing, sea parks, fur, leather, down, wool)		trapped in jobs in which they must inflict pain upon animals.
Political dysfunction (e.g., corruption, gerrymandering, money in politics, lack of free and fair elections, disenfranchisement)	All	• Many so-called democracies around the world are in name only, without free and fair elections and led by dictators and oligarchs. • In the US, money in politics, corporate lobbying, redistricting/gerrymandering, voter disenfranchisement, distrust of the election process, falsehoods about voting legitimacy, etc. have resulted in a political system that is not working effectively and does not always represent the majority.

After the reflections you've done thus far reading this book, and having considered the problem chart above, take time to choose an issue to explore that captures your heart and mind and compels you to want to learn and to act. Then dive into your research. Search the Internet, listen to (reliable) podcasts, read (reputable) news reports, and bring your critical thinking to everything you uncover. From the research you'll be conducting, you will narrow down a problem to an aspect you can successfully address. When you do this, it will be best if you've chosen a problem that makes sense for you at this time.

As a reminder, you do not have to choose what you think is the biggest problem in the world (unless, of course, it's the one that most deeply tugs at your heart and gets the wheels of your mind spinning). Nor do you have to choose a problem that others around you—whether family, friends, members of your spiritual community, or neighbors—care about.

It does not have to be a problem covered regularly in the news. It should simply be meaningful to *you*.

Identify the problem you want to solve

To give you a sense of how you might narrow a big issue into a specific, local problem, the following chart uses the same list of problems in the preceding chart with three examples of local manifestations for each problem. This chart is meant to offer a few examples to help you to focus on a narrow enough problem to address as you go through the next phases of the solutionary process. (Again, this chart is simply an example,

BIG PROBLEM	LOCAL MANIFESTATIONS
Climate change	• Personal/city/regional energy not from renewable sources • Carbon-intensive foods served in home, local school, workplace, church/synagogue/mosque, hospital, etc. • Lack of convenient public transportation options and/or biking paths in my community
Poverty	• Poverty, homelessness, and hunger in my community • Lack of access to quality, affordable healthcare in my community • Lack of access to good jobs and affordable higher education/technical education in my community
Modern-day animal agriculture (factory farming)	• Factory-farmed products served in my home, local school, workplace, church/synagogue/mosque, hospital, etc. • Lack of education in my community about the impacts of factory farming so that people can make informed dietary choices • Few laws to protect farmed animals in my state
Isms (racism, sexism, classism, ableism, etc.)	• Lack of education in my school/workplace/church/synagogue/mosque about how to address and solve one (or more) of these structural problems where it occurs in my community • Polarization around whether to even discuss these problems in my community and in my local schools

BIG PROBLEM	LOCAL MANIFESTATIONS
	• Lack of legislation/policies to address local or state forms of structurally embedded isms
Animal cruelty (trapping, hunting, poaching, fishing, animal experimentation, trafficking, poisoning, rodeos, circuses, horse and dog racing, sea parks, fur, leather, down, wool)	• Roadside zoo, sea park, animal racing (dog or horse), trophy hunting, or other animal "entertainment" in my community • Rodeo or circus coming to town • Cruel wildlife control programs in my state or community
Political dysfunction (e.g., corruption, gerrymandering, money in politics, lack of free and fair elections, disenfranchisement)	• Gerrymandering is happening locally and impacting fair elections • Politicians in my state are working to disenfranchise voters and make voting harder • Clean election laws, ranked choice voting, and other efforts to create a healthier democracy are missing in my city and/or state

and you'll find a much longer, combined version of the two charts in appendix 4.)

Write down a problem statement

Whether you choose a problem from the list above, one that's personal and impacting your life right now, one that you've been concerned about for some time, or one you've recently identified through your inquiry and research, write down a problem statement. Your problem statement should be a concise description of the problem you wish to solve. The following are examples of some problem statements:

- My family produces too much trash.
- A local factory is polluting the air and water in my neighborhood.
- There is limited access to affordable housing in my city.
- Overdose deaths are on the rise in my county.
- Loopholes in my state's animal cruelty laws allow for the legal mistreatment of farmed animals.

Phase II: **Investigate**

4. Connect with everyone you can who has a stake in the problem, including those working to solve it
5. Determine the causes of the problem
6. Research what has succeeded and failed in solving it

In Phase II, Investigate, you'll become a careful researcher. You'll learn from a range of stakeholders and discover who and what is harmed and who and what benefits from the problem you're addressing and the systems that perpetuate it. You'll uncover the causes of the problem and investigate what's already been done to solve it. It is in this phase of the solutionary process that you will be practicing and honing your critical and systems thinking skills so that you'll be ready to develop a solutionary solution in Phase III.

Connect with everyone you can who has a stake in the problem

Stakeholders[66] include all those who have a "stake" in an issue. When we think of stakeholders, we generally think of people who have interests in the outcome of decisions. In the solutionary process, stakeholders refer to everyone and everything that is affected by a problem: obviously humans, but also other animals and elements of our biosphere.

The more we connect with those who are affected by the problem we hope to solve, the more nuanced our understanding of the problem and its impacts will be and the greater the chance that we'll solve the problem in as MOGO a way as possible. We'll also develop a deeper appreciation for what's already been done to solve it, better understand the outcomes from those efforts, and discover what's been learned by others in the process.

We can't ask other species or ecosystems about the impacts of a problem on them directly, of course, but we can ask those people who've been advocating for and working to protect animals and the environment, as well as people who are benefiting from actions that harm other species.

Because of the era in which we live, where global communication is relatively easy, if we choose to address a problem far removed from us, for example, a refugee crisis elsewhere in the world, the trafficking of wild animals for the exotic pet trade, or rainforest destruction, we can still connect with stakeholders. With that said, remember that starting locally usually makes more sense as you are developing your solutionary skills.

Stakeholders can be people who are:

- personally impacted by the problem and/or understand the impacts on other species and ecosystems; (Note: if you choose a problem that is impacting you, your family, and/or your community, you are a stakeholder. Make sure to ask yourself the questions you will be asking other stakeholders and experts.)
- likely to be impacted positively by potential solutions and are therefore invested in solutionary thinking and action; and/or
- potentially impacted negatively by possible solutions (i.e., they may lose money, power, land, resources, et cetera) and may therefore be opposed to change and/or fear personal negative consequences.

It's very important to talk to people in the category described in the third bullet above. To be a solutionary is to strive to develop solutions that have the fewest unintended negative consequences, which means we must understand the impacts of a solution on those who will lose out if it is effectively implemented. It's virtually impossible to ensure that everyone's competing interests will be met fully, but to the degree that we seek out, listen to, and attempt to understand all stakeholders' interests, we can develop solutions that aim to do the most good and least harm for everyone.

You are likely to have greater success in engaging the support of those who may face negative impacts from your solutions if some of their concerns are met. For example, those who might respond badly to low-income housing units being built in their neighborhood or a potential wind farm that they feel will mar their personal view (often derogatively referred to as NIMBYs, short for "not in my backyard") may be more willing to engage with solutionary efforts if they are brought into the process of addressing and solving the underlying problems as respected stakeholders, rather than as perceived selfish adversaries.[67]

Privileged NIMBYs already have a voice in our society, coupled with the power to advocate for their interests, so while it's very important to talk to these stakeholders, we need to remember that it is the most marginalized people, not the wealthiest, whose neighborhoods are usually the sites for unwanted projects, including those that may ultimately have a solutionary goal. While most people recognize that it is unethical to build polluting factories, farms, mines, et cetera in low-resourced communities where neighbors (and ecosystems) then suffer health consequences from poorly regulated pollutants, we need to pay attention to the complexities that arise when it is a solutionary effort that leads to industrial activity. For example, batteries for energy storage require ores that are procured through mining that is often polluting, an unintended negative consequence of a well-intended shift. Much of that mining occurs in poorer countries, making it easier for those in wealthier countries to ignore that these mines are situated in someone else's backyard, often in places where people have little or no means of resistance when the mines are built without attention to human rights and environmental impacts. When we don't see or hear from these people or seek out their perspectives, it is all too easy to forget that they are stakeholders whose interests should be considered and whose health and safety should be protected, along with that of other species who may be affected.

In my own state of Maine, there is a history of mines polluting the water in low-income communities, and dedicated, solutionary-minded people have successfully advanced laws that ban open-pit mining of more than three acres in our state. But now we are faced with a new situation requiring more nuanced solutionary thinking. In a recently publicized example of our current quandary, a couple discovered that their large rural property has the "richest known hard rock lithium deposit in the world."[68] Lithium is a key component in energy storage and other green technologies, but excavating this rich lithium source may not be possible because of Maine's strict mining law, even though the couple own thousands of acres and the mining could be carefully engineered in an environmentally and socially responsible way. This couple has no desire to despoil the environment. They are also eager to support clean energy.[69] Given that the demand for lithium is growing as we advance technologies to replace fossil fuels, is preventing mining on their property still the best answer, especially since this means continuing to outsource lithium mining to less protective countries and less protected communities? Might responsible mining in this low-populated region be preferable to the out-of-sight-out-of-mind procurement of lithium mined elsewhere? What's the solutionary way?

As Phil Coupe, managing partner at ReVision Energy, wrote, "If we are able to extract Maine's lithium deposits in a way that is not environmentally destructive, then I think we have a tremendous opportunity to help accelerate the transition to renewable energy + storage while strengthening Maine's economy."[70]

This is all to say that learning from stakeholders requires digging below the surface and employing the thinking skills and MOGO principle that you're cultivating throughout the solutionary process.

EXAMPLES OF PROBLEMS AND STAKEHOLDERS

PROBLEM STATEMENT: There is lead in my city's municipal water.

STAKEHOLDERS WITH WHOM TO CONNECT:

- families impacted by lead poisoning
- healthcare professionals
- teachers and school administrators where students suffer from lead poisoning
- city engineers and planners
- state legislators and city council members
- insurance companies
- organizations and individuals working to solve the problem on a local and/or national level, especially those who've successfully addressed and solved the problem in their own region

PROBLEM STATEMENT: Dogs and cats are being killed in shelters in my state because they lack homes.

STAKEHOLDERS WITH WHOM TO CONNECT:

- homeless dogs and cats (at shelters and rescue organizations)
- shelter personnel, especially those who euthanize dogs and cats
- breed rescue groups
- pet store and puppy mill owners and breeders
- people who purchase purebred or designer[71] puppies and kittens
- organizations and individuals working to solve the problem on a local and/or national level

When talking to those who are harmed

When talking to those who are harmed by the problem (or who represent those who are harmed in the case of problems that impact animals and the environment), you'll want to ask questions to understand the ways they are affected and what they want to see change. Make sure to listen with compassion. If you are talking to parents whose children have brain damage from lead in their water or shelter workers who have to endure the daily task of killing healthy animals because there aren't enough people adopting them, you are likely to encounter painful emotions along a spectrum that may include intense sorrow and/or fury.

Since you have chosen to address the same problem yourself, you're likely to experience a range of painful emotions, too. This will obviously be even more pronounced if you've chosen to address a problem that's causing you and your family harm. Use these emotions as fuel to make a difference, and remember that in Phase II you are gaining insight and knowledge so that you can solve the problem, which will help relieve those painful emotions for everyone.

When talking to the beneficiaries

When talking to those who are benefiting from what you consider to be a problem (as well as the systems that perpetuate it), remember you are there to learn, not to express judgment. This can obviously be challenging, but this is your opportunity to put on your solutionary lenses and practice listening and understanding. It may be wise to reach out to those who are opposed to change *before* reaching out to those who are negatively impacted by the problem. If we wait until after we have heard from and deeply empathized with those suffering from the problem, we may be full of so much anger and sadness that we cannot contain our judgment. This may make it difficult to ask respectful questions, listen effectively, and bring a solutionary mindset to the problem. If you are addressing a problem that is harming you and/or your family and community personally, it can be emotionally detrimental (and possibly physically unsafe) to dispassionately reach out and speak with beneficiaries of the problem and the systems that perpetuate it. You might want to partner with others who face fewer personal risks who can talk with beneficiaries and report back to you or your group.

When you talk to people who do not see the problem the way you do and who are benefiting in some way from the status quo, you'll want to ask them politely and sincerely how they perceive the problem. Do they recognize that it is a problem for others? Do they think it is a problem worthy of concern? Would they like to see the problem resolved in ways that do the most good and least harm for everyone affected? If so, what changes might they be willing to make or countenance to achieve a positive result?

Let's say you are addressing the problem above concerning dogs and cats being killed for lack of homes. You may have strong feelings about the purchase or breeding of purebreds and designer pets because you understand that other animals will suffer and die as a result of people buying and breeding dogs and cats within a country where there are more pets than there are homes for them. When you talk to a breeder, a pet store owner, or someone who bought a purebred, be cognizant that your job is to better understand their perspectives in order to be able to find leverage points for solutions that will be widely embraced and successfully adopted.

While it's easy (and often comes all too naturally) to judge people, your efforts to learn and understand may backfire if you are judgmental.

Remember that people don't wake up in the morning thinking, What can I do to cause harm and suffering today? Often people lack information or the will to make different choices. For example, people who have purchased purebred or designer pets practically always adore them and want the best for them. They may not have realized the potential negative impacts of purchasing a dog or cat from a pet store or breeder and contributing to a society where there are more pets than there are homes. It's also possible that they know about pet overpopulation but the supply and demand calculation feels so distant and indirect that they don't consider the role they play. They may have wished to raise an animal from puppyhood or kittenhood and have not been able to find puppies and kittens at their local shelter, or have been so attached to a certain breed that they let that attachment eclipse concerns about animals killed in shelters. They may have worried about behavior problems that sometimes accompany older rescued animals, not realizing that behavior problems can occur with a purchased puppy, too. But even if they are benefiting from the system that produces more pets than homes, chances are they love dogs and cats, just as you do, and don't want them to be killed. They might even be eager to find solutions to the problem of pet overpopulation. It's possible that they'll have some good ideas for you to consider if you are respectful and open as you seek to learn and understand.[72]

When talking to experts

As part of the process of investigation, you'll be reaching out to people with experience addressing and working to solve the problem. These days it's relatively easy to find contact info for such people online. Connecting with them is an exciting part of the solutionary process. When you talk to people with expertise, you might ask:

- What do you think are the systemic and root causes of the problem?
- What are the impacts of the problem and the systems that perpetuate it?
- Who is benefiting from the status quo?

- Why does the problem persist even though so many people recognize it as a challenge to be solved?
- What successes and/or failures have you experienced trying to solve this problem?
- With whom have you collaborated to solve it?
- Whom else should I learn from?
- When this problem is solved, what do you predict will have been the most significant factors in achieving success?

Remember that when you connect with people who have expertise around the problem you're addressing, by definition they will have a bias. Just as you are carefully evaluating information for accuracy and bias when you conduct research, make sure to do so when you speak with stakeholders who have been working to solve the problem. Experts are not immune from and may have even greater cognitive biases, and they may have more difficulty than neophytes remaining open to differing perspectives.

You may also find it helpful to seek success stories from those who've solved a different but potentially relatable or analogous problem and/or who have experience leveraging the same system for change. For example, if you anticipate the need to work with city council members to solve your problem, you may wish to connect with others who've successfully worked with your city council in the past.

Determine the causes of the problem

Although you'll be asking people with experience working to solve the problem to share what they consider to be its causes, you'll need to do your own research. Determining the causes of a problem can be like trying to trace a spider web, because there are typically multiple, intersecting causes rather than a single cause. Exploration of one cause may lead to another. A combination of inquiry and investigation will uncover even more layers and connections, and soon interconnecting systems will appear. These systems didn't arise spontaneously and don't exist in a vacuum. They are informed and driven by a variety of other causes including psychological and biological factors, worldviews, beliefs, values, and mindsets.

The iceberg model

The image of an iceberg can be helpful in understanding these layered causes, which is why many systems-change organizations use an iceberg model to help people become better systems thinkers. The model that we use at the Institute for Humane Education is a modification of others we've seen. It is somewhat of a simplification to make it easily accessible and understandable to everyone, even those with no systems-thinking instruction or background.

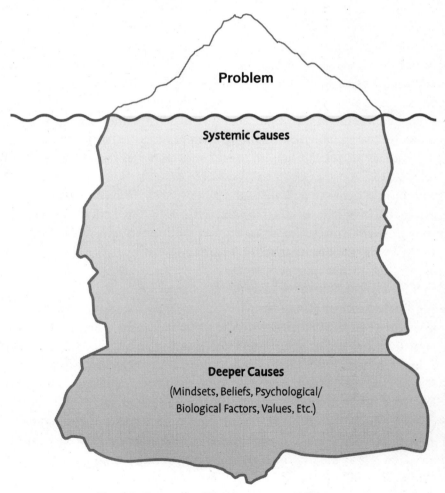

Fig. 5.2: Credit: Zoe Weil. Illustration: MJ Jessen

At the top of the iceberg, above the surface of the water, lies the problem. The problem didn't emerge out of nowhere of course; it had causes. The phrase "it's just the tip of the iceberg" refers to the fact that the majority of an iceberg is hidden below the surface. Just as we can see the tip of the iceberg poking out above the water, so too can we see problems. What we can't see—unless we take a deep dive (metaphor intended!)—are the interconnected causes and feedback loops that have created the problem and that perpetuate it. Unless we look below the surface and address the causes, we're not going to be able to stop the problem from persisting.

For example, let's say the problem we want to address is litter in our neighborhood. We can easily see the problem. We can even address the problem by cleaning up the trash ourselves or organizing larger community efforts to do so. But if we don't uncover the causes of the litter, we'll be picking up trash forever. We will never solve the problem until we change the systems and mindsets that perpetuate it.

Systemic causes

In the iceberg model, the societal systems that have led to the problem lie hidden beneath the surface. In the case of litter, there are many such systems:

- our **production and economic systems** that produce disposable products and packaging of no value to consumers, and which are therefore readily discarded
- our **education and parenting systems** that fail to reinforce our role as stewards of the planet
- our **legal and policing systems** that are unable to reliably identify and hold accountable litterers in order to deter future littering
- our **media systems** that have not inspired or compelled everyone to stop littering and care for the commons
- the lack of trash receptacles (**design systems**) in cars and along streets and roadsides, making it less convenient to bring trash to where it can be disposed of responsibly

What deeper, or root, causes for littering might we add to our iceberg? Here are some:

- laziness and aversion to inconvenience
- "out of sight, out of mind" attitude
- apathy
- selfishness
- myopia
- lack of respect for the environment
- lack of respect for the commons
- "it's someone else's problem" mindset

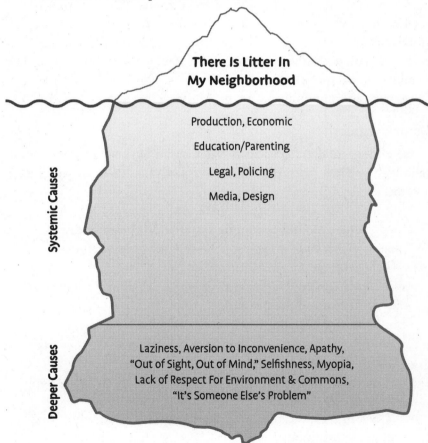

Fig. 5.3: Credit: Zoe Weil. Illustration: MJ Jessen

As a child growing up in New York City, at a time when approximately 40% of adults smoked cigarettes, it was common to see people throw their butts on the ground. Cigarette butts littered the streets, but it seemed as if they were not perceived as litter by those who tossed them on the ground. The same people who threw their butts on the ground wouldn't necessarily be likely to throw other trash on the ground. To do so would be unacceptable, even in their own eyes.

When I was in middle school, if I saw someone toss their cigarette butt on the sidewalk, I sometimes picked it up, walked up to them, and said, "Excuse me, I think you dropped this." (Yes, on many occasions I was that snarky, holier-than-thou tween.) While this was hardly a solutionary approach to a long-standing problem, it did elicit some noticeable embarrassment among the litterers, which is to say that the butt-throwers usually realized that what they were doing might be wrong. Could we cultivate an understanding that the commons should be protected, not despoiled? Could this cause be one we should leverage for change? We'll get to leverage points for creating change in Phase III, but notice that it won't be uncommon for your mind to jump straight to solutions as you identify causes, so you'll want to save the immediate ideas that pop into your head for later when you are working to develop solutions.

Asking why

A problem I've been addressing and trying solve for much of my career is this:

Most US public schools are not educating
their students to be solutionaries

To dig deeply into the causes of this or any problem, it's helpful to ask the question "why?" as in: *Why don't most US public schools educate their students to be solutionaries?* Initial "why" questions lead to research. In my case, my research led me to seek out the mission of the US Department of Education, and I discovered that it is "to promote student achievement and preparation for global competitiveness."[73] I also explored the history of compulsory schooling, its goals, structures, and curricula.

Through this research and investigation, more "why" questions arose, such as:

- Why is global competitiveness a primary goal of US schooling when it is not the primary goal of students, teachers, and parents?
- Why don't we make the curriculum truly relevant to students' interests and needs; allow students to pursue the questions that most interest them; and apply literacy, numeracy, the scientific method, research, and other academic skills to the task of addressing those issues of greatest personal concern to students?
- Why do we divide the core subjects we teach into the four categories of math, science, language arts, and social studies, and why do we divide daily units of instruction into short, specific, and predictable time periods of approximately 45 minutes, none of which has any clear relevance to the others, so that teaching and learning are rarely interdisciplinary and often feel haphazard to students?
- Why do schools still use textbooks rather than rely on the most up-to-date information, lessons, units, and exemplar curricula, as well as primary sources and state-of-the-art software?
- Why are debate teams so ubiquitous in US schools, while teams dedicated to solving the problems that underlie debate topics are so rare?
- Why has the public school system changed relatively little despite so many societal, technological, scientific, economic, and geopolitical changes?

Each "why" question led to more research, which led to more "why" questions, which led to more research. What was revealed through this process were many interconnected systems.

In 2022, I convened a group of long-time public school teachers, curriculum developers, and administrators to collaboratively complete the iceberg model around the problem statement: *Most US public schools are not educating their students to be solutionaries.* The systems we collectively identified that contributed to the problem included:

- the public education system
- university schools of education that prepare future teachers
- federal and state departments of education
- economic systems
- political systems
- legal systems
- media systems
- construction and production systems
- food systems

Asking more questions, doing more research, and relying on our collective experiences led to uncovering subsystems within those systems. For example, asking why the K-12 school system has changed relatively slowly despite rapid societal and technological changes led to subsystems within education and revealed potentially outdated approaches, such as:

- **Slow-to-change teacher training programs** within university education departments. Because teachers cannot teach what they don't know, haven't been taught, and haven't been mandated to learn, teacher training programs that don't incorporate real-world, solutions-focused education will leave future teachers unprepared to educate their students to be solutionaries.
- **Instructional models that favor direct instruction,** which is easier to manage and grade than independent and problem-based work that is harder to plan for and assess.
- **Lack of awareness about exemplary curricular material,** which, coupled with entrenched relationships with textbook publishing companies, means that teachers don't know where

to find solutionary units, modules, software, or approaches to bring to their students.

- **Lack of assessment studies** demonstrating the positive impacts of solutionary learning on students' critical and systems thinking capacities; literacy, numeracy, research, and communication skills; statistical analysis abilities; scientific literacy; engagement with learning; mental health; compassion; and sense of hope and efficacy. Without such studies that show positive results, there are fewer incentives to change the system.

- **Long-standing practices with corporations that produce standardized tests,** coupled with testing mandates, that lead to "teaching to the test." We generally teach what is evaluated, and the sense of urgency to improve public education continues to center on improving math and reading scores. This means that identifying and meeting the many other needs of today's learners, as well as opportunities for more relevant learning, are often pushed aside.

- **College admission requirements** that have been slow to change such that high schools continue to funnel strong students toward meeting traditional distribution requirements even though those requirements may no longer be in the best interests of those students or their future.

- Failure to grapple with the **very purpose of school** in such rapidly changing times, which creates confusion about what content and skills ought to be taught and through what pedagogies.

Within both the media and political systems we identified subsystems that lead to either/or thinking and away from solutionary thinking, which seeps into school culture and pedagogy. For example:

- **The media is complicit in either/or thinking** because binary analysis is encouraged by journalists who write stories in which, for the sake of balanced reporting, they seek "both sides," as if there are only two ways to think about complex issues and as if "both sides" have equal weight. Moreover, sensationalized either/ors that encourage side-taking grab our immediate attention, while nuanced thinking, perspective-taking, and collaborative problem-solving tend to require more time, thought, and engagement than is typically cultivated by the media or politicians.

- **The media and politicians frequently create "manufactured problems,"** which divert our attention from real problems. For example, the outcry about transgender students using the bathroom of their gender identity is a manufactured problem since there is no evidence that allowing trans youth to use the bathroom associated with their gender identity results in a lack of safety.[74] (The fact that transgender kids have high rates of depression and suicidality is, however, a real problem.[75])

- Through legislation and policies, **political systems mandate both what is and isn't taught in schools.** In many states, not only has science been under attack for many years, but political and media systems have also combined to spark "culture wars" that lead to polarization around actively promoted and vastly over-hyped controversies. To avoid criticism and conflict, school boards, school administrators, and teachers tend to shy away from these controversial topics, which diminishes the opportunities for teaching solutionary thinking that would serve as an antidote to polarization by bringing together groups to research, investigate, learn from each other, and collaborate to solve agreed-upon problems.

- **The US Department of Education's mission statement** hasn't changed since its inception in 1979. Given the enormous changes we've undergone that affect young people and their future opportunities and responsibilities, the entrenchment of what many consider to be an outdated mission impacts what is and isn't taught.

How we design schoolrooms, buildings, and campuses impacts the learning that happens within them. Within the construction and production systems, we identified:

- **architectural subsystems** that produce school buildings that are indoor- and classroom-based and keep students separated by age and subjects, remove elements of nature that could otherwise be integrated into the curriculum, and are often not welcoming, exciting, beautiful places to be, think, learn, and innovate; and
- **school furniture subsystems** that often keep students in individual desks that are unidirectional facing the teacher, which can then lead to lecture-style teaching pedagogies rather than research-focused and collaborative approaches.

These furniture and architectural subsystems are reinforced by the subsystem of teacher training and professional development mentioned earlier which do not generally focus on preparing teachers to individualize the curriculum, promote collaborative learning and problem-solving, or focus on real-world issues, all of which would be antithetical to the physical structure of learning in rows of desks facing a "sage on the stage" in a calcifying instructional system.

At first it might seem like a stretch to connect food systems to education systems. For most people, there isn't an obvious connection, but as one of the educators participating in this analysis, sixth-grade World Studies and Language Arts teacher, Julia Fliss, queried: *What do students see and learn from the foods that are served in the school cafeteria every day?* I've already discussed food systems in this book, but it's worth unpacking Julia's question in the context of examining subsystems that perpetuate potentially outdated traditions and diminish solutionary approaches in the classroom.

What might we discover?

- **What's served in many school cafeterias,** from the high-fat, low-fiber, sodium-laden, and animal-based meals, to disposable plates and utensils, to the high-sugar content in what comes out of the vending machines, is often in direct conflict with what students are or should be learning in health, biology, ecology, and environmental science classes.

- **Schools are required by the federal School Lunch Program** to provide students with cow's milk (that taxpayers subsidize), even though an estimated 36% of Americans are lactose intolerant after early childhood and wind up with digestive problems by consuming dairy products that they do not need and that are not healthful for them.[76]
- **The Dairy Council,** an arm of the dairy industry, has been supplying nutrition curriculum to schools for decades that are essentially advertisements for dairy products rather than science-based nutrition recommendations from trained nutritionists and healthcare professionals.

—⁓—

What are the deeper causes that have led us to create the systems and subsystems that are resulting in US public schools not educating students to be solutionaries? Some of the "why" questions earlier hint at deeper causal elements, but there are more why questions to ask, such as:

- Why doesn't the teaching profession in the United States confer much status? This isn't the case everywhere. For example, in Finland teaching became a high status job when the country invested in teacher preparation, funded master's degrees for future teachers, and began attracting the top 15% of college graduates, making teaching a highly competitive career choice.
- Why are so many teachers leaving, or planning to leave, the profession, and why is the attrition rate for new teachers so high?[77]
- Why don't teachers get paid more, given that their work is so essential to ensuring a thriving future, they work such long hours, and they have so much responsibility?[78]

- Why don't teachers and administrators embrace the solutionary approach as soon as they learn about it, not only for the sake of their students and the future but also as a corrective to polarization?

The more why questions we asked, the more the deeper causes—mindsets, values, worldviews, belief systems, and psychological factors—began to reveal themselves. These "why" questions, coupled with the personal experiences of the educators and administrators in our group who were completing the iceberg analysis, led us to fill in the "deeper causes" section of the iceberg and include the following:

- fear of controversy/conflict
- inertia
- lack of imagination
- lack of leadership
- lack of rewards/incentives for doing more than is required
- confusion about what is a basic or necessary skill
- lack of societal focus on prevention in general (education is the ultimate prevention)
- lack of autonomy and respect
- desire to retain power and be the authority in the classroom
- desire to conform
- crisis/reaction mindset
- complacency (lack of motivation to learn new approaches)
- exhaustion/overwhelm/burnout
- fear of being fired or reprimanded
- denial that there's a problem

Find the connections

The next step is to identify those systems, subsystems, and deeper causes that are connected to one another, which we can do by drawing lines between them on our iceberg. Almost always, when looking for these connections, it becomes evident that virtually all the systems and causes are linked. While our iceberg is now a visual mess, seeing these interconnections and then *identifying the relative strength of these connections* is helpful when it is time to identify leverage points for change in Phase III.

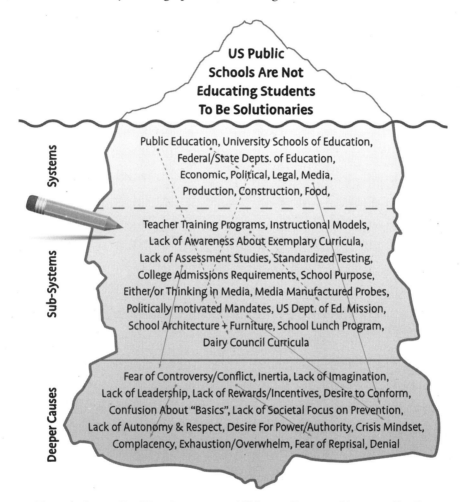

Fig. 5.4: CREDIT: ZOE WEIL. ILLUSTRATION: MJ JESSEN, PENCIL BY YURLIC ON FREEPIK

What questions should we ask other than why?

"Why" questions aren't the only questions to ask of course. We also need to ask "who" and "what" questions. In turn, these may help to identify ever more probing "why" questions.

For example:

Who...

- determines school, district, and state missions for education?
- writes new curricula and guides schools to implement them?
- educates the educators?
- coaches new teachers and those who are struggling in the profession?
- determines the criteria for becoming and assessing a teacher, curriculum designer, principal, and superintendent?
- determines what constitutes acceptable continuing education credits/units for teachers?
- writes the standardized tests upon which students and schools are evaluated?
- determines what's required for college admission?

What...

- is missing in current curricula both in terms of content and pedagogy?
- prevents schools from embracing new approaches to education that are innovative and relevant both to students and to their era?
- would inspire more college students to pursue the teaching profession?
- can we let go of in the existing school curriculum to make room for solutionary approaches?

—⁓—

I hope the example above demonstrates the complexity and interconnectivity of both systemic and deeper causes. I also hope that your mind is churning with your own questions and that you are eager to jump into (or continue) your investigation of the problem you want to solve.

While tracing the spider web of causality can be challenging, it is essential. Only when we take the time to investigate the interconnected root and systemic causes of problems will we be able to choose effective leverage points to solve those problems in a solutionary way.[79] The questions you'll ask to ascertain the causes of the problem you're addressing will lead you in many directions, and your research will inevitably reveal intersecting systems and create a clearer picture that will make your solutionary efforts more effective.

Begin with a "quescussion"

As implied above, if we want to solve problems, we need to ask the right questions. To fire up your mental muscles to do the research you'll need to do, I invite you to find a friend, family member, or colleague who cares about the problem you've identified and who's willing to participate in a quescussion, an activity developed by Paul Bidwell at the University of Saskatchewan to promote higher-order questioning skills. I was introduced to this question-focused activity by Dr. Mike Johnston, a teacher, international school leader on the forefront of sustainability education, and the first graduate of our doctoral program. During the activity, Mike had us pair up and instructed us to have a discussion about a problem conducted solely through questions. We could ask *any* question in response to our partner's question, but we could *only* ask questions. Our answer to our partner's question? Another question.

The quescussion was a bit awkward as we groped for another question as a response to our partner, with longish pauses in between. It was also revelatory. Forced to only ask questions, we dove deeper and deeper into the problem. We unveiled layers of querying and thinking that would later lead us to more effectively and thoroughly examine the issue under quescussion.

In the context of polarized issues in our society, a quescussion can help us move from knee-jerk side-taking to more nuanced thinking. And in relation to big challenges like climate change, a quescussion can lead us toward leverage points for systemic change.

Here's what a quescussion might sound like around the problem of misinformation and disinformation in our society.[80] Let's imagine the quescussion is between two friends, Aisha and José:

Aisha: How can we distinguish between misinformation, disinformation, and truth?

José: How can we ever really know what's true?

Aisha: Why is it so difficult to change our minds when the evidence is so strong?

José: What would help people to be more open and less attached to their beliefs?

Aisha: What would help people think critically about information they hear, read, or see?

José: Whom do you trust?

Aisha: Whom do *you* trust?

José: Why do you trust them?

Aisha: Does mistrust breed more misinformation and disinformation?

José: How many times have I shared misinformation myself?

Aisha: How can we break the cycle of increasing misinformation and disinformation?

José: Are misinformation and disinformation actually increasing or do we just think they are?

Aisha: Was misinformation and disinformation more or less common 20, 40, or 60 years ago than it is now?

José: How could we find out the answer to that question?

Aisha: When photos, videos, and voices can be faked, how can we ever know what's true without deeply investigating everything, which would be impossible?

José: Can today's technological tools that enable misinformation and disinformation to spread also be used to ascertain truth?

Aisha: Might we soon have AI that can instantly provide truthful, fact-based answers to our questions?

José: What verification systems would need to be in place to trust such AI?

Aisha: Is trust declining?

José: If trust is declining, could that inspire more critical think-
           ing and truth-seeking?

Aisha: Could declining trust lead to more confirmation bias and
           belief in disinformation?

José: Why are people so susceptible to cognitive bias and to
           misinformation and disinformation?

Aisha: What can I do to make myself less susceptible?

José: What steps can I take to ensure that I don't spread misin-
           formation and disinformation?

Aisha: What steps can we take to help others do this as well?

See how much is revealed through this quescussion, and how the
"conversation" touches upon core questions that can ultimately lead to
essential research and investigation, deeper understanding, and more
powerful responses to the underlying problem?

To conduct your own quescussion, set a timer for ten to twenty minutes
and record the quescussion so you can listen to it and notice insights and
direction for pursuing answers to the challenges you face. After listening to
your quescussion, note those questions that you believe are most important
to pursue in order to find solutions to the problem you seek to address.

There's a reason why I chose the problem of misinformation and disinformation when describing the quescussion. As you conduct research
to ascertain the answers to the many questions that will arise as you seek
to understand the causes of the problem you are addressing, make sure
to practice your critical thinking skills, along with the CRITIC method
described in chapter 3, to ensure that you are obtaining the most accurate information possible. Until and unless we have trustworthy artificial
intelligence (AI) systems that provide accurate information (which Aisha
and José inquired about in the quescussion), it's up to us to be vigilant
in our fact-checking.

Research what has succeeded and failed at solving the problem

It's rare to choose a problem that no one else has sought to solve, so
there's a good chance you've chosen a problem that others have already

worked on. All of the problems listed in appendix 4 have been reported in the news and tackled by social entrepreneurs; nonprofit organizations; governments, legislators, and policy-makers; educators; activists, changemakers, and community organizers; and numerous experts in a variety of professions from engineering to law to healthcare. Nonetheless these problems persist.

When speaking with stakeholders experienced in addressing the problem, you'll be learning about what's already been done to solve it, but just as you have to deeply investigate the root and systemic causes of the problem yourself, even though you asked expert stakeholders for their opinions about causes, you also have to thoroughly investigate what's been done to solve it.

While it should be obvious that doing this research is essential, when we have fire in the belly to do something, and do it now, the pull can be strong to bypass this step. There are two things to keep in mind as motivation for taking your time to do this research carefully:

- There's no need to reinvent the wheel if good solutions exist that simply need other good solutions for effective implementation.
- It's important to avoid solutions that have already been found to be less effective than expected or that have been shown to have significant unintended negative consequences.

Often, there is growing awareness about a problem and growing public sentiment for solving it, but the increase in human population coupled with rising income levels means that the problem may be getting worse despite greater concern about and dedication to ending it. Climate change is an obvious example of this. So is animal suffering within meat, dairy, and egg production. This is true for many problems, which suggests that proposed and implemented solutions need to become ever more solutionary.

Sometimes solutions languish in obscurity because the innovator of a solutionary idea may not be as good at communication or expansion (sharing and scaling) as they are at innovative thinking. Sometimes organizations miss opportunities for collaboration and therefore diminish the impacts they could have if instead they worked together toward their common goal and amplified their efforts. Great solutions to challenging problems already exist that address climate change, poverty, political dysfunction, animal cruelty, et cetera. Your role as a solutionary may be to help make these solutions become better implemented through leveraging the right systems in the right ways.

By carefully researching what's been done to solve the problem you're addressing, analyzing the successes and learning from the failures, and paying attention to any unintended negative consequences from different approaches that have been tried, you'll gain the knowledge you need to take your next steps as a solutionary.

For example, consider the persistent conflicts between humans and coyotes. For more than a century, the typical approach to address these real and/or perceived conflicts has been lethal. Whether in urban or agricultural areas, the traditional response to the presence of coyotes has been to trap, shoot, or poison not just the "offending" coyote, but often all of the coyotes in the area. Obviously, this is not a solutionary approach, since to be solutionary a solution needs to do the most good and least harm for people, animals, and the environment, and killing coyotes doesn't take their interests into account.

Moreover, this approach has generally been both ineffective and counterproductive, leading to more, rather than fewer, coyotes in the region. This is because indiscriminate killing often results in compensatory reproduction, meaning coyotes compensate for the reduction in their numbers both through increased litter size and pup survival, as well as breeding at a younger age. Coyotes refill any territorial vacancy quickly.

With this information about failed solutions in mind, more and more communities are recognizing that a solutionary way to reduce or eliminate conflicts between people and coyotes lies in public education and the adoption of coyote coexistence plans that address the root causes of the conflicts (often unprotected food sources), and which focus on behavior modifications for both people and coyotes.

Since coyotes can provide a needed ecological service in both urban/ suburban as well as agricultural regions by keeping rodent and rabbit populations in check, learning how to live *with* rather than *in opposition* to coyotes means everyone can benefit.[81]

What makes this example particularly useful for illustrating this step in the solutionary process is the combination of learning what's been tried in the past, along with bringing a solutionary lens that seeks to avoid solutions that harm one group (coyotes) to help another (people). The solutionary lens, coupled with scientific evidence about failed approaches, can lead to the adoption of more solutionary solutions.

Phase III: Innovate

7. Develop solutions that address the causes of the problem, avoid unintended negative consequences, and do the most good and least harm to people, animals, and the environment
8. Decide which solutions are most solutionary and most feasible for implementation
9. Draft a plan to implement your solution

You've explored. You've learned. You've researched. You've brought your critical and systems thinking to bear on your problem. Now you're ready to think strategically and creatively and devise solutions in Phase III, Innovate.

Develop solutions that address the causes of the problem, avoid unintended negative consequences, and do the most good and least harm to people, animals, and the environment

There's a well-known story about the World Health Organization (WHO) trying to solve the problem of malaria in Borneo in the 1950s. The solution was to spray DDT to kill the mosquitoes that carried the parasite that caused the malaria outbreak. The DDT worked to reduce malaria, but it also killed the wasps that controlled populations of thatch-eating caterpillars, so before long there were holes in the thatched roofs of dwellings. Holes can be patched, so that would have been a manageable unintended negative consequence, but then the island's cats started dying. The theory is that the cats died due to high levels of DDT that became concentrated in their bodies through the food chain. With the reduction in cats on the island, the rat population increased, which then resulted in an outbreak of plague because the rats carried the fleas bearing the bacteria that caused the disease. In other words, trying to solve one disease outbreak led to another disease outbreak. That's quite an unintended negative consequence! The response of WHO was to parachute crates of cats into Borneo to solve the problem of too many rats.[82] "We don't want to parachute cats" is a refrain we might repeat to ourselves so that we avoid the potential unintended consequences of our own solutions to the problems we seek to solve.

Finding leverage points

In chapter 3, I mentioned the importance of finding strategic leverage points when seeking to devise a solution. Were it not for the many unintended negative consequences (that extended far beyond the cats and rats in Borneo), DDT could have been a great leverage point to solve the problem of malaria. If it had *only* affected the malaria-carrying mosquitoes, perhaps DDT as an insecticide would have been a powerful solutionary innovation.[83] In fact, during the first couple of decades of its use, its success at limiting the spread of insect-borne diseases led to its discoverer, Paul Hermann Müller, being awarded the Nobel Prize in Physiology or Medicine in 1948. Only later did scientists uncover the ways in which DDT impacts many other animals and ecosystems. For example, the population of Bald Eagles, the national bird of the United States, began to decline when DDT moved up the food chain into their bodies causing them to lay eggs with thin shells that broke during incubation or failed to hatch at all. DDT also kills beneficial insects like bees and is suspected of being a human carcinogen.

Systems thinking expert Donella Meadows wrote in her article "Leverage Points: Places to Intervene in a System": "[Seeking leverage points] is not unique to systems analysis—it's embedded in legend. The silver bullet, the trimtab, the miracle cure, the secret passage, the magic password, the single hero who turns the tide of history. The nearly effortless way to cut through or leap over huge obstacles. We not only want to believe that there are leverage points, we want to know where they are and how to get our hands on them. Leverage points are points of power."[84]

Meadows goes on to write that leverage points are not always intuitive and can systematically worsen whatever problems we are trying to solve if we are not careful (as in the DDT example). Because of highly complex and interconnected societal systems that intersect with biological systems, we have to be very cognizant of unintended negative consequences as we assess possible leverage points and possible solutions. There is no foolproof method for doing this. Avoiding unintended negative consequences requires thinking through the range of possible scenarios that might follow the implementation of a solution so that we avoid parachuting cats. This is why cultivating good systems thinking skills is so important for solutionaries. We simply can't avoid such consequences if we aren't able to recognize the interconnecting systems that will be affected by our solutions.

In the iceberg model, effective leverage lies below the problem level. There can be leverage points at the systems level and at the deeper causal level of mindsets, psychological factors, beliefs, and values. As mentioned earlier, we can pick up trash on streets and alongside roadways, but we will never solve the problem of litter unless we leverage the systems, mindsets, and psychological factors that cause the problem to persist.

Asking "how" questions

To ascertain the causes of problems we ask lots of "why" questions, plus some "who" and "what" questions. To determine solutions to problems, we need to ask "how," as the answers will help us think about where to find leverage points. "How" questions have likely already arisen during your quescussion. In Phase III of the solutionary process, you'll give them more of your attention.

Let's say the problem you're addressing is the rising rates of type 2 diabetes among children in the United States, an issue mentioned in chapter 1. A first "how" question might be: How can we reduce the rate of type 2 diabetes among youth in the United States?

This question will lead us to look at the systemic and deeper causes in our iceberg model, which we would have completed during Phase II. Our iceberg (minus the connecting lines) might have looked something like this:

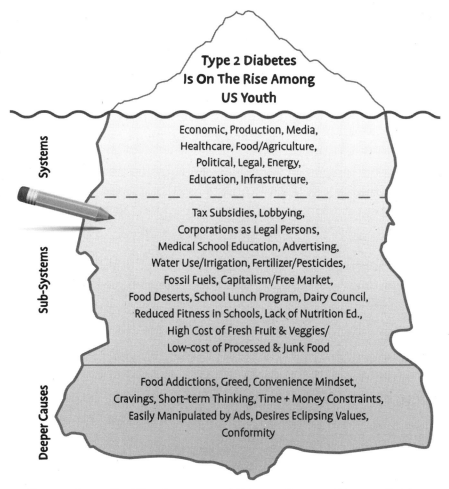

Fig. 5.5: CREDIT: ZOE WEIL. ILLUSTRATION: MJ JESSEN, PENCIL BY YURLIC ON FREEPIK

As we look for leverage points where we might devise solutions, we're going to want to find those leverage points that will have the biggest impact. Intuitively, we may want to choose leverage points at the deepest causal level, believing that they will have the most far-reaching effects. For example, if kids just stopped craving refined carbohydrates (e.g., cakes, cookies, chips, sodas, candy) and certain kinds of meat,[85] type 2 diabetes would likely decline, but would a campaign to get kids to stop craving (and then eating) these foods be the most strategic approach? Probably not. This is because there's a biological reason why we crave fatty, sweet, and salty food, and it's extremely difficult to change our biological impulses through willpower alone. The "just say no" approach doesn't tend to succeed when biological and psychological factors are urging us to say yes. We will likely realize this as soon as we ask *how* we can get kids to stop craving (and then eating) foods that lead to diabetes. We will likely discover we need to ask some other "how" questions, such as:

- How can we agree on a definition of healthy and unhealthy foods?
- How can we reduce kids' access to unhealthy foods?
- How can we increase kids' access to foods that are healthy?
- How can we stop externalizing and subsidizing the costs of unhealthy foods?
- How can we make sure healthy foods are affordable?
- How can we ensure the School Lunch Program provides healthy foods?
- How can we enable and motivate families to adopt healthier diets?
- How can we make sure that kids have more opportunities for exercise and fitness?

And (remembering our quescussion) how can we continually ask the right "how" questions so we can find simple, effective leverage points and solve the problem in a solutionary way?

Some of the "how" questions above will lead us to leverage the systems that have perniciously capitalized on the deeper causes. We might leverage:

- **Political, agricultural, and economic systems,** which shift the true costs of unhealthy foods so that the least healthy foods have also become the least expensive to purchase.
- **Legal and advertising systems** that permit advertising of unhealthy foods and beverages to children.

THE FOUR PHASES OF THE SOLUTIONARY PROCESS 115

- **Economic, government, and city planning systems** that have turned some neighborhoods into fast food and convenience store meccas where affordable nutritious foods are harder to come by.
- **The National School Lunch Program**—enmeshed in the agricultural, political, and economic systems—which has led to many schools becoming repositories for high-sugar, high-fat, and processed foods, accustoming children to poor eating habits from a young age.

As we think about leverage points, we'll need to evaluate the likelihood of successful solutions to the problems we're addressing based on several factors:

- the potential impact of the leverage point
- the feasibility of the solutions at that leverage point
- the impact of the forces that may propel the solutions forward
- the impact of the forces that might thwart the solutions

It's important to consider more than one leverage point and more than one solution per leverage point.[86] Doing so helps us learn how to strategize, make effective decisions, and become more successful solutionaries. It's also important to recognize that there are feedback loops between the systems level and the deeper causes. As mentioned earlier, *when systems change, mindsets, values, and beliefs often follow.* Change is not unidirectional.

To avoid pursuing those solutions that could have unintended negative consequences, make sure to consider all the interconnected systems that will be impacted by your solution and ask yourself:

- Might vulnerable people be harmed by my solutions?
- Are there potential negative impacts on ecosystems that might arise as a result of my solutions?
- Could sentient animals suffer due to my solutions?

It's important to try to identify all the potential harms so that when it's time to choose which solution to implement, you'll be able to choose the one that's most solutionary.

What solutions might we devise at the different leverage points in relation to the question: How can we reduce the rate of type 2 diabetes among youth in the United States?

We might work to:

- recommend and pass legislation that stops subsidies for unhealthy foods, while simultaneously working to pass legislation that subsidizes fresh fruits and vegetables so they are widely accessible;
- recommend and pass legislation outlawing the advertising of unhealthy foods to children;[87]
- overhaul the School Lunch Program so that only healthy foods are served to students and ensure these foods are free or at reduced cost for all in need;
- partner with supermarkets to donate produce they would otherwise throw out because it doesn't look up to par;
- partner with farms to donate produce they would otherwise throw out because it's the wrong size or shape;
- eliminate junk food, fast food, candy and cakes, soda, sweetened beverages, and much of the meat served in schools[88] in schools, children's hospitals,[89] community centers, and other places where children have access; and
- include daily, accessible, and fun exercise and fitness programs in schools that don't exclude kids who may not excel at competitive team sports and/or who have disabilities.

Let your creativity flow

This step in the process is also where you'll want to let loose your creativity. While I've focused primarily on using strategic thinking in this phase to identify effective leverage points, remember that this process can and should be creative. There's no reason to hold back on ideating a range of solutions, however out of the box they may be. In the next step, you'll choose which solution to pursue, so it's useful to have thought as creatively as possible in step 7. You might use the suggestions on pages 61-62 in chapter 4 to jumpstart your creative thinking. Innovative ideas may arise just from giving yourself permission to think in a creative way.

Determine which solutions are most solutionary and most feasible for implementation

There are many factors to consider when it comes to implementation. Your most solutionary ideas may not be the ones that you are able to implement because of time, resources, support, and expertise; however, it is helpful to identify the most solutionary solutions anyway, even if you are unable to implement them yourself. Perhaps other people you know will have the ability to implement one of your ideas. Maybe you'll write or speak about a solution, and some reader or listener will be inspired to make it a reality.

Remember that it's possible to choose a solution that someone else has come up with but which hasn't yet become widespread and isn't being implemented as it could and should be, or which hasn't been implemented in your community. Your most solutionary solution may be to bring it to your region and/or offer new approaches for expanded implementation and scaling of others' ideas.

Here is a graph to help you evaluate the solutionariness of your solutions:

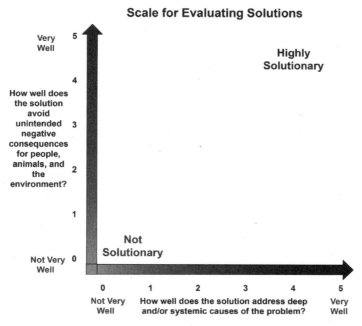

Fig: 5.6: *Solutionary Scale.* CREDIT: INSTITUTE FOR HUMANE EDUCATION BY KACEY DEWING.

Once you have your handful of solutionary solutions, you can create a chart or spreadsheet to determine what solution will ultimately be the most solutionary for you to pursue. Your chart should include the following:

Possible solution	Where does the solution fall on the solutionary scale?	Who/What benefits from the solution?	Who/What could be harmed from this solution? (What are possible unintended negative consequences to people, animals, and/or the environment?)	Is the solution feasible for me to implement?	What time and resources are necessary to implement this solution?	Do I want to pursue this solution? Is it a good use of my talents?

Taking the time to go through all the solutions you've generated and complete your chart helps tremendously when choosing which solution to pursue and implement. You may find that it's helpful to return to those experts and stakeholders with whom you spoke in Phase II to ask for feedback on your ideas. You can then use their input as you decide which solution to pursue.

If you are working together with friends on the same problem—which is a great way to embark on your solutionary practice—it's possible that you'll want to pursue different solutions. Instead of all working on one solution, you might work on several, and then share your experiences and what you learned with each other, like various departments in a solutionary organization. There may be exciting synergies that arise as your group takes different approaches to solve a problem.

Draft a plan to implement your solution

In this final step in Phase III, you'll create a plan to implement your solution, but before you do, it's helpful to reflect upon and record your long-term goal. Ask yourself what it will look like when your long-term goal is achieved. How will things have changed? How will people, animals, the environment, and/or you benefit? What will define success?

Next, record your short-term measurable objective(s). Depending upon the problem you've chosen to address, your long-term goal may not be achievable in the near future, but your measurable objective(s) should be.[90] For example, your long-term goal might be a more democratic society; your feasible solution might be to inspire and register young people to vote or to challenge voter-suppression in your community or state; and your short-term measurable objective might be an increase in voter turnout in your community or state.

Perhaps your long-term goal is to reduce greenhouse gases in the atmosphere; your feasible solution is to work with neighbors, friends, and local legislators to draft and pass legislation in your city to reduce fossil fuel use by a certain percentage; and your measurable objective will be the change in fossil fuel consumption in your municipal buildings and schools (rather than the overall reduction of greenhouse gases in the Earth's atmosphere). Or maybe your feasible solution is to implement an educational program to help families and businesses in your community reduce their carbon footprint. Your measurable objectives might include how many people were exposed to your program and the concrete steps they took to act on what they learned.

The next step is to reflect upon what things are like right now, before you begin implementing your solution. This is the "baseline status." You'll want to know where your starting point is as you plan your action steps to create change so that you will be able to measure success.

Below is a suggested chart to help you document your long-term goal, your measurable objective(s), and the baseline status.

Long-term Goal:	Measurable Objective(s):	Baseline Status:
• What's my big vision and hope?	• What specific changes will have occurred relative to my long-term goal? • How will I measure success?	• What does the problem I'm addressing look like now, before I begin implementing my solution?

Now it's time to complete your planning chart, using the headings below and writing down all the action steps you can think of, no matter how small, so you can be strategic and methodical in your process and best address challenges as they arise.

Action steps (Be specific)	Individuals involved (Including stakeholders)	Resources needed (If applicable)	Timeline (Date by which the action should be completed)	Potential challenges (What could derail your plans?)	Ideas to address potential challenges (Consider asking expert stakeholders)

Phase IV: Implement

10. Implement your solution
11. Assess and share your solution
12. Celebrate and iterate

It's time to put your solutionary thinking and planning into action. If you've carefully completed Phases I-III, you're now ready to ensure that the fruits of your efforts lead to positive changes in Phase IV, Implement.

Implement your solution

Implementing your solution is an ongoing process that may occur over weeks, months, or years, depending upon the complexity of the problem you're addressing. If you have gone through the three previous phases in the solutionary process (Identify, Investigate, and Innovate), chosen a feasible solution with measurable short-term objective(s), and completed your planning chart, you are ready to make your solutionary idea a reality.

Assess and share your solution

As you implement your solution, it is important to honestly and regularly evaluate your outcomes. Are you meeting your measurable objectives? Are you avoiding unintended negative consequences? Are systems and/or mindsets actually changing? Has your implementation been truly solutionary, or has it been more humanitarian in practice as discussed on page 20–21?[91] Are you asking your stakeholders how your solution is affecting them? If your stakeholders aren't humans, have you determined how to answer this question on their behalf, and are you carefully assessing your results?

This step is also a time for introspection. Did you choose a leverage point that enables you to capitalize on your skills and interests? For example, if you've engaged in politics at the local level to advance new legislation, ask yourself if the political system is a leverage point you want to stick with to address another problem at the state or national level. If so, wonderful! If not, switch levers. It's important that you enjoy the solutionary process and that you make the best use of your skills.

If your solution is going well and there are positive outcomes, you'll also want to share these as widely as possible so that your ideas spread and are adopted for greater impact. But even if things aren't going as well as hoped, it is valuable to share what you've learned with others so they can avoid the mistakes you've made and the pitfalls and challenges you've experienced. Sharing what you have learned educates others, which is solutionary in and of itself because education sparks others' solutionary thinking and actions.

Celebrate and iterate

Solutionary work isn't easy. It requires deep thinking, commitment, discipline, and sustained effort. As you achieve your goals, including any stepping stone objectives on the path toward bigger successes, make sure to celebrate and to include stakeholders in your celebration.

Last but not least, consider how you can increase your positive impact. Ask yourself how you might refine your ideas. What can be iterated so that your solutions are improved upon and/or extended? For example:

- If your efforts have led to a shift in your workplace that has resulted in a healthier and more humane HR policy, how can you advance similar goals in other workplaces?
- If you made headway in transforming some of what's served in your local school's cafeteria but hit roadblocks that prevented

you from fully achieving your goals, what are the next steps to negotiate those roadblocks?

- If you created a workshop to bring people together across divides, build bridges, and reduce polarization and side-taking, have you provided participants with an evaluation form through which they can give anonymous responses so that you can improve the workshop with their feedback in mind?
- If you've successfully worked to pass legislation that prevents the dumping of manure and sludge that's been polluting soil, air, and water in your community, what steps can you take to ensure that the new law is enforced?

———

My hope is that the four-phase solutionary process you've just learned about seems more exciting than daunting. Remember that being a solutionary is not all or nothing. Nor is the solutionary process an either/ or proposition. It's a mindset, a lens, a way of thinking, and a path. If you've read this far and embarked on the process of solving a problem in a solutionary way, then you are a solutionary. And if you're wondering how solutionary thinking and action are being manifested within various societal systems, the next chapter will highlight some solutions that are currently taking root or appearing on the horizon.

Chapter 6:

SOLUTIONS

T HIS FINAL CHAPTER IS meant to provide some examples and ideas
for transforming systems rather than to be thorough, detailed, or
directed toward specific problems such as war, climate change, poverty, et
cetera. Many other books have been written that focus on these specific
problems and offer meaningful solutions. As one example, *Regeneration*
by Paul Hawken, along with its accompanying website, Nexus,[92] offer
comprehensive solutions to end the climate crisis in a generation.

A few of the solutions I'll describe are taking hold deeply and already leading to meaningful systemic change, while others are further
from significant adoption. Virtually all are interconnected even though
I am writing about them under separate headings. Some are small shifts
that could have big impacts if they are extended and supported by other
changes within intersecting systems. A couple of them are especially solutionary. Artificial intelligence (AI), a solution which recurs in several of
the following sections, offers tremendous opportunities to help solve a
host of problems, but it simultaneously presents grave risks if we do not
develop it carefully and in a solutionary way.

There are many more systems I could have included (e.g., energy,
healthcare, media, defense, infrastructure, et cetera), but the goal of this
chapter isn't to provide an overview of all the emerging systemic solutions
to all the problems we face (which would require many more books).
Rather, it's to focus on a few large systems and a few proposed ideas within
each.

You'll notice that these solutions fall into different categories of action
and approach. Some are legislative or policy changes. Others are technological or design innovations. Some are educational.

This chapter just touches the surface, and I offer it less to promote any specific solutions than to remind you that solutionaries abound and are working, and often succeeding, at solving problems. I hope this chapter gives you some ideas for your own solutionary efforts as well as a dose of evidence-based optimism.

Food Solutions

Food has come up a lot in this book because of all the systems we depend upon, it may well have the most far-reaching negative impacts.[93] The 2005 Synthesis Report of the United Nations' Millennium Ecosystem Assessment describes agriculture as the "largest threat to biodiversity and ecosystem function of any single human activity."[94] Logically, then, if we transform our food systems in solutionary ways, we will build a sustainable and humane world that much more rapidly.

To summarize and add to some of the points I've already made in this book, current industrial food production, which is highly reliant on animal agriculture and its concomitant monoculture feed crop production:

- requires prodigious amounts of land, water, and fossil fuels;
- is an extreme polluter of water;
- is one of the biggest contributors to climate change;
- leads to significant soil erosion;
- depends upon large quantities of environmentally destructive pesticides and fertilizers;
- leads to ocean dead zones;
- has been implicated in both zoonotic diseases and antibiotic resistance;
- is responsible for continuing deforestation, especially in rainforests;
- is cruel to animals; and
- is exploitative of people.

As I've also already mentioned, one of the most pernicious problems exacerbating our current destructive food systems is the persistence of subsidies for foods that are unhealthy, inhumane, and produced in non-regenerative, unsustainable ways. Many organizations[95] are working to shift subsidies away from destructive practices and toward healthy and sustainably and humanely produced foods, addressing problems within food, political, economic, and legal systems simultaneously.

As George Monbiot writes in his book *Regenesis: Feeding the World Without Devouring the Planet,* "Crops should be grown for food, not to produce animal feed, fuel, or bioplastic."[96] He goes on to say, "The systems we should favor are those that deliver high yields with low environmental impacts. The systems we should reject are those that deliver high yields but with high environmental impacts, or low yields."[97] With this in mind, if we can reduce the land required to feed humanity, we can return it to an ecologically flourishing state with restored habitats that simultaneously reduce carbon in the atmosphere.

Solutionaries who are focused on food issues are developing new systems for growing crops directly for human consumption that nourish the soil instead of erode and poison it. One of the more exciting solutions Monbiot describes in his book is the development of perennial grains— plants that produce food for several years. Currently, virtually all grains, whether produced for direct consumption, animal feed, or biofuels are annuals that require tilling, fertilizers, and pesticides each year, which contributes to soil erosion and pollutes land and water. Perennial grains require much less fertilizer and herbicide, maintain soil health, sequester more carbon, grow in marginal land, use soil nutrients more efficiently, and grow for a longer period of time.[98]

But to truly reduce land use, we need to transform how we produce our primary sources of protein. The belief that people need animal products to obtain enough protein is a myth that's been hard to dispel. Vegans are constantly asked, "Where do you get your protein?" even though it's virtually impossible to become protein deficient on a diet of grains, legumes, nuts, seeds, and vegetables that meets one's caloric needs.[99] For athletes whose protein requirements are higher than the average person, it is still easy to get enough protein on a plant-based diet.[100] Nonetheless, the myth persists, and for various reasons, and despite an ever-growing number of people adopting plant-based diets, most people seem unwilling to forgo meat, dairy, eggs, and sea animals even if they don't need to eat them. As we know, habits, desires, and belief systems are hard to shift.[101]

But solutions are emerging that will enable people to have their cake and eat it too, though in this case they'll have their meat and eat it too. In addition to plant-based meats, some of which taste virtually identical to and with similar protein levels as meat from animals, food scientists and many emerging companies are developing cultivated meat.[102]

Cultivated meat is animal meat produced by growing animal cells rather than raising and killing animals. Hundreds of companies and academic laboratories are working on developing affordable cultivated meat. Early assessments indicate that cultivated meat will use 99% less land and vastly less water and energy than current animal agriculture.[103] It will also eliminate animal suffering and animal waste. In addition, cultivated meat is produced entirely without antibiotics and doesn't carry the risk of zoonotic disease outbreaks and animal-to-human pandemics. Once produced at scale and at a price point comparable to meat from factory farms, it can quickly replace slaughterhouse meat.

A highly cost-effective protein source that requires even less energy than cultivated meat, as well as no antibiotics or pesticides, is fermentation-derived microbial protein from microorganisms such as fungi, bacteria, and algae.[104] Although the name may sound off-putting, people already happily consume fungi (mushrooms) and fermented foods with bacteria (e.g., miso, cheese,[105] and yogurt[106]). The sky's the limit for the culinary opportunities for this protein technology.[107]

The reality is that if we want to feed billions of people while restoring ecosystems, we simply have to move away from animal agriculture and vast monoculture feed-production. The emerging new solutions to do so may sound suspicious to those of us who've grown up with the picture-book images of bucolic farms inhabited by happy animals who live in harmony with the Earth, but those images don't represent our current reality, while the horrific impacts of today's practices are all too real. While there are still some small, organic, picture-book farms, they produce a tiny fraction of the animal products people consume. Given the land and labor involved, it is not feasible for such farms to supply the quantity of meat, dairy, and eggs to fulfill the current (and growing) global demand.

As mentioned earlier, while it can sometimes be hard to change mind-sets and belief systems directly (and hence to inspire everyone to adopt a plant-based diet), the development of new systems that become integrated into societies and supermarkets will inevitably shift values and perspectives. Solutionaries in food production are accelerating this inevitable change. In the future, the vast majority of us will likely be eating protein that is not derived from raising and slaughtering animals, and, just as likely, we will rue the past where we despoiled our environment, trawled our oceans, and caused so much animal suffering.

Population Solutions

In the 1970s, population growth was a significant concern, especially in the wake of the Club of Rome's report, *The Limits to Growth*,[108] and Stanford University professors Paul and Anne Ehrlich's bestselling book, *The Population Bomb*,[109] that predicted mass starvation if population growth continued on its precipitous trajectory. Population has more than doubled since then, but agricultural production and calorie consumption have more than kept pace. A vastly smaller percentage of people suffer from a lack of food today despite the continuing increase in population. Ironically, a growing percentage of people now suffer from excess calories and the health impacts that ensue from consuming too much food.

When the book's dire predictions of widespread famine didn't come to pass due to the Green Revolution in farming—which, unfortunately, has had profoundly destructive unintended negative consequences to the environment despite its success at producing enough food to feed a growing human population—the book was widely criticized, and concerns about overpopulation began to diminish. The Ehrlichs were also criticized for focusing on population growth in poor countries, even though the great majority of individuals in those countries had a much lower ecological footprint than people in wealthier countries.

When coercive policies to lower birth rates followed in the wake of population concerns, the worthy goal of reducing population became conflated with human rights violations.[110] Then, when the rate of population growth began to decrease, worries began to diminish that our population would grow indefinitely.

The primary reasons why the rate of population growth has declined are because poorer countries have become wealthier, more girls have been able to go to school, and access to family planning has increased. These shifts result in women delaying childbirth and having fewer children.

These days it's now common to see news reports bemoaning declining birth rates. With an aging population in numerous countries, leaders and economists in many nations express worry that there will not be enough people in their workforce to provide the tax funding necessary to care for the needs of their elderly citizens. In response, some governments are now pressuring and incentivizing women to have children.

While the growth *rate* has declined, the overall human population continues to increase with incontrovertibly negative impacts. While it's true that we have discovered methods to increase food production to feed this growing population (albeit through means that continue to be highly destructive), more people results in more land and resources required to sustain a larger population. With a greater number of people across the globe moving out of poverty and into the middle class,[111] there is a higher demand for consumer goods, vehicles, energy, building materials, meat, et cetera, which leads to more resource depletion, pollution, habitat destruction, and animal suffering.

Few people deny that it's unsustainable to have an endlessly growing population. After all, our planet is finite, and the prospect of colonizing other planets anytime soon is far-fetched, even for a *Star Trek* fan like me. Yet many are convinced by current trends that:

- population growth will stabilize naturally, and overall population will begin to decline, which will solve these problems, and/or
- the decline in population growth will become a serious threat to economic stability and forebode a bleaker future.

It is ironic indeed that concerns about population have shifted from alarmism about population growth to alarmism about population decline. Like so many issues explored in this book, this should not be an either/or. Both create problems, and these problems can be solved in solutionary ways. We can address the challenges of declining population growth while supporting those efforts that advance women's autonomy and the ensuing reduction in human population that leads to more stable and thriving ecosystems.

To reduce population, the most solutionary solutions have been and are likely to continue to be those promoted by groups such as Population Balance,[112] which include:

- **Education,** particularly for girls and women who, as mentioned above, are more likely to delay marriage and childbirth and have fewer children if they are able to attend school. As an example, the decline in Bangladesh's birth rate from 5.5 children in 1985 to 2.1 children in 2017 is largely attributed to the education of girls and women.[113]
- **Access to family planning** so that women and their partners can make better-informed decisions about the number of children they wish to have and avoid unwanted pregnancies.
- **Improved maternal and child health,** which reduces infant mortality and results in women having fewer children overall.
- **Government policies that support population reduction,** such as incentives for delayed and smaller families (the opposite of the trends we're currently witnessing).
- **Norm-shifting strategies,** such as mass-media soap operas/ telenovellas and radio dramas that reach hundreds of millions of people and, through entertainment, shape social norms around reproductive awareness, gender equality, and fertility.[114]

To support our aging population, other solutions must come into play, such as:

- **Encouraging healthy lifestyle choices** and preventive healthcare measures to help older people stay healthier and reduce the need for intensive and costly medical care.
- **Investing in healthcare and social services** for the elderly such as home care, assisted living facilities, and geriatrics.[115]

- **Supporting intergenerational communities** that integrate
  people of different ages to provide opportunities for older people
  to stay engaged and active and receive community support.
- **Developing technology-based solutions** such as telehealth,
  robotics, and artificial intelligence, which can be used to provide care and support to older people in cost-effective and
  innovative ways.

Economic Solutions

I would need another book, and much greater expertise, to address and
share truly solutionary solutions to the problems within and connected
to economic systems. In this section I will share a few ideas that, along with
other systems changes (especially in the areas of production and politics),
can help get us closer to building healthy economies that do as much
good and as little harm as possible.

First, I want to address our tendency to use overarching terms like
"capitalism" and "socialism," both to critique and advocate for solutions
to the problems caused by and within these economic systems. Often,
we do not carefully define what we mean when we use these terms, and
side-taking can lead us away from solutionary thinking. Below are brief
definitions of these terms.

- Capitalism advocates for market-driven production, distribution, and exchange of goods and services through private
  ownership, with the goal of creating a prosperous economy
  through competition and the pursuit of profits.
- Socialism advocates for collective ownership and control of the
  means of production, distribution, and exchange of goods and
  services, with the goal of building equitable, healthy societies.

Despite the distinctions between these definitions and goals, the reality is that few, if any, economic systems and nations are entirely capitalist
or entirely socialist. Almost all exist along a spectrum between the two.

Capitalism dominates the world's economies, but even in the United
States not all goods and services are privately owned. Government programs

like Social Security, Medicare, Medicaid, and public K-12 education and public libraries are operated for the public good, while roads, bridges, state and national parks, the postal service, and police and fire departments are also government-operated and not privately owned. Other government-run agencies include the military and the Veterans Administration, the National Aeronautics and Space Administration (NASA), the National Institutes of Health (NIH) and National Science Foundation (NSF), the Federal Emergency Management Agency (FEMA), the Federal Aviation Administration (FAA), Federal Highway Administration (FHWA), Federal Communication Commission (FCC), the judicial system, and state health departments, social service agencies, and state emergency management programs, among others. The US government also makes enormous tax-funded investments in the innovation, development, and spread of technologies that have significant social benefits. NGOs and nonprofit organizations also provide a social good not motivated by profit.

Many nations that are commonly perceived, and sometimes referred to, as socialist are not actually practicing socialism as their dominant economic system as defined above. The Nordic countries are periodically described as socialist, but they are social democracies that combine capitalism with generous social safety nets and services, such as universal healthcare, free primary, secondary, and higher education, affordable (or subsidized) childcare and preschool, paid parental leave, and social welfare supports to ensure housing and a basic standard of living to everyone.

What varies considerably among nations is the balance of taxation and redistribution of wealth, regulations and protections for people and the environment, and social services, not to mention the political structures in which these economic systems are embedded, which vary dramatically and include democracies, oligarchies, totalitarian regimes, monarchies, and military dictatorships.

No country has built a perfect economic system (and reasonable people disagree about what a "perfect" economy would look like), and no country can extricate itself from the others given the interconnected nature of economies. Problems abound in every nation's economy to greater and lesser degrees. In many countries, poverty is a persistent problem, as is sweatshop labor and the enslavement of adults and children in various industries. In some nations, the primacy of individual freedom and private ownership leads to greater inequities and damaging monopolies. And pollution, habitat destruction, and animal abuse persist in virtually all large-scale economies, regardless of the overarching political-economic system within which they operate.

Solutions to the local and global problems that economies create and perpetuate, as well as models for alternative approaches to production and distribution, are constantly arising, being implemented, and being iterated within individual countries' contexts. For example, many socially minded economies exist within their larger capitalist-oriented structures. In the United States, these include cooperatives for food, housing, and businesses, credit unions for obtaining capital, public power utilities that supply electricity to approximately 15% of US citizens,[116] and municipal water (upon which most people in the United States rely).

Not all economies-within-economies are small scale. The Mondragon Corporation, a network of worker-owned cooperatives based in the Basque region of Spain, comprises more than 250 businesses and employs nearly 75,000 people, making it one of the largest worker-owned cooperatives in the world and the seventh largest company in Spain. The members of each cooperative elect their own management and share in the profits of the business.

What Mondragon demonstrates is that a workplace can be a setting where democracy is welcome and practiced, which is rare among businesses (whether they are run privately in capitalist systems or by governments in socialist nations). It's important to note that while democracy, cooperation, innovation, worker participation, shared profits, and social responsibility are core values of Mondragon, this does not mean that everything they produce is humane or sustainable. Much of it is not. Nor are Mondragon companies willing or able to control many of the negative externalities associated with their businesses because they exist within larger globalized systems. Negative externalities refer to costs not borne solely (or perhaps at all) by the producer of those effects but by others. Examples include air pollution from factories, rainforest destruction for cattle grazing, and the Great Pacific garbage patch, an area in the

Pacific Ocean that is bigger than Texas and which is full of plastic. While Mondragon owners don't currently control their negative externalities, imagine what might happen if the worker-owned employees voted to commit to solutionary production that does the most good and least harm for everyone? Such workplace democracy could well lead to profound solutionary changes.

Some countries are considering a basic income to ensure that everyone's essential needs are met. The overall benefits include reduced poverty, increased entrepreneurship by providing a safety net to pursue new ideas and ventures without the fear of financial ruin, and simplified bureaucracy and lower administrative costs for welfare benefits. While supplying a basic income is costly and controversial, since the second half of the 20th century, it has variously been championed in the United States, first by the Nixon administration, along with Democrats and Independents to this day. With the potential of new technologies and AI increasing productivity and profits while also potentially causing millions of people to lose their jobs, a basic income could be an antidote to the unintended negative consequence of what is often referred to as "progress"—as long as it doesn't cause serious unintended negative consequences itself.

Nuanced solutionary thinking about how to build economic systems that do the most good and least harm for all people as well as other species, and which ensure environmental sustainability, is essential. And we will have to address the inherent problems associated with economic growth. Defined as an increase in the production of goods and services in an economy over time, economic growth is perceived not only by the majority of economists but also by most people as a largely unmitigated good. Economic growth can lead to higher income levels and improved access to education, medical care, and better living conditions, all of which can contribute to greater longevity and health. Economic growth is often a measure of technological innovations, new job creation, and increased employment opportunities, which in turn increase tax revenues that, with supporting political efforts, can then fund public services and infrastructure, including the kinds of infrastructure needed to shift to a clean energy economy and support elderly populations.

But there's a serious downside to simply focusing on economic growth. It is inextricably linked to greater production and consumption—currently inseparable from resource depletion, habitat destruction, and pollution—which are primary drivers of inhumane and unsustainable activities. Economic growth is also unlikely to lead to greater income equality and often has the opposite effect, increasing inequity when profits and income are not widely distributed.

Economic growth is generally measured by gross domestic product (GDP), which doesn't distinguish between economic activity that is inherently positive and that which follows harms and catastrophes. For example, it doesn't distinguish between economic activity that's a result of building new solar panels and economic activity to rebuild communities devastated by climate change-caused fires, hurricanes, and floods. It doesn't distinguish between software advances that allow people across the globe to access innovative educational opportunities and increased sales of prosthetic legs to replace the limbs of soldiers who have been injured in wars.

As Esther Duflo and Abhijit V. Banerjee write in their book, *Good Economics for Hard Times*, "When a tree gets cut down in Nairobi, GDP counts the labor used and the wood produced, but does not deduct the shade and the beauty that are lost. GDP values only those things priced and marketed." In other words, economic growth by itself simply doesn't measure increased well-being. This means that we must carefully assess how much benefit economic growth is actually providing. To be a measure of genuine progress, economic growth should not be associated with economic activity that is the result of or causes harm.

Below are a few solutions that address some of the downsides of economic growth specifically, as well as capitalism in general. As you read about each, consider where you think it falls on the solutionary scale. If it were scaled up and/or better promoted or enforced, what positive systemic impacts might it have?

- **The Genuine Progress Indicator (GPI):**[117] This metric measures the well-being of a nation, region, or city by incorporating environmental and social factors which are not included in GDP. By replacing or supplementing GDP with the GPI, we could pursue overall well-being, not simply growth. The GPI takes into account a range of factors, including the distribution of income and wealth, the value of unpaid work such as caring for children or elderly relatives, the cost of crime and pollution, and the depletion of natural resources.

The GPI is calculated by subtracting the negative impacts from GDP (e.g., crime, environmental degradation, resource depletion, income inequality, etc.) and adding the positive contributions that are not captured by GDP (e.g., the value of unpaid household, volunteer, and community work). The resulting figure provides a more comprehensive and nuanced view of well-being than GDP alone.

Many states, nations, and communities are using such metrics to measure and improve overall well-being, including Maryland and Vermont, which have implemented a GPI, Canada, which uses the Canadian Index of Well-Being,[118] and the Organization for Economic Cooperation and Development (OECD), which created the Better Life Index.[119]

- **The Code for Corporate Citizenship:** Robert Hinkley, a former corporate lawyer, proposed the Code for Corporate Citizenship to amend the duty of corporate directors "to act in the best interests of their corporations" by adding the following words, "but not at the expense of severe damage to the environment, human rights, public health and safety, dignity of employees or the welfare of the communities in which the corporation operates."[120] To be a viable solution, this idea would need to be adopted on a national scale so that companies could compete on a level playing field. With political will to implement such a code, we could balance the pursuit of economic growth with overall well-being and ensure that measures were in place to prevent or limit the harm such growth can cause. (I would personally add to the code language to prevent cruelty toward animals as well.)
- **Doughnut Economics:** English economist Kate Raworth has proposed Doughnut Economics as a model for building

economies that are sustainable, equitable, and socially just.[121] The name comes from the image of a doughnut, with its outer ring representing ecological limits and the inner ring representing the minimum foundation needed for a good life. The goal of the model is to find a balance between these two rings.

The primary principles of Doughnut Economics include a focus on meeting the basic needs of all people (e.g., access to food, water, healthcare, education, and housing), living in an ecologically sustainable manner, addressing inequality, and promoting social justice. To be a successful model for corporations and governments, defining the parameters of the doughnut and ensuring compliance within those parameters is key to its value as a framework for economies. (Again, I would add living in a humane manner toward animals to the doughnut model.)

- **Regulations:** We rely on governments to mitigate the negative impacts of economic systems through regulations. We can and must make sure that these regulations:
  - prevent monopolies
  - ensure that corporations pay the full cost for their use of the commons
  - disallow companies from causing significant pollution and/or habitat destruction
  - require that corporations treat people justly and animals humanely
  - protect consumers from fraud, false advertising, price gouging, and predatory lending
  - prioritize safety when developing new technologies, products, and medicines
  - impose tariffs on unsustainably, inhumanely, and unethically produced goods from other countries
  - set up a scorecard on all the factors above for transparency, and so that those companies that do more good are rewarded and those that cause harm are transformed positively or eliminated

To the degree that regulations are necessary, fair, have clear compliance measures, are efficient in their administration, and are enforced, they are critically important levers for building economies that work for all.

Production Solutions

Our economic systems cannot be separated from our production systems, which cannot be separated from the advertising and marketing systems that are endlessly encouraging us to buy more and more stuff. For those of us with incomes that exceed what is necessary to meet our basic needs, much of what we buy is nonessential. Look around you right now. How much of what you see are things you like or want but do not actually need? When we do research in the True Price activity (described on pages 57–58), we discover that most things we purchase carry a cost to other people, animals, and the environment. The endless production of stuff has serious consequences.

But what if we could produce the products we both need and desire without the ensuing harm? How might we decouple production from environmental destruction, child and sweatshop labor, slavery, animal abuse, and other forms of exploitation and injustice? How can we advance production that's helpful while preventing production that is harmful?

This is an arena where solutionary solutions exist in theory but have yet to become practiced at scale because to be implemented they need a combination of political, economic, and technological support to be viable within a market-driven economy. While some aspects have been adopted by some companies (e.g., embracing fair-trade policies for labor), other aspects have not (e.g., ensuring that the product's entire lifecycle is regenerative and produces no waste).

In their book *Cradle to Cradle: Remaking the Way We Make Things,* William McDonough and Michael Braungart ask us to think beyond "cradle to grave," which describes the lifecycle of virtually all of our products, and instead—taking a cue from the natural world—make products "cradle to cradle," meaning they are not simply less toxic, less wasteful, and more recyclable but entirely regenerative and circulate within a closed loop of nutrients.

In the cradle-to-cradle model, all production materials fall into one of two categories of nutrients: "technical" or "biological." Technical nutrients are nontoxic synthetic materials with no negative environmental effects and which can be reused in perpetuity. Biological nutrients are organic, healthful materials that can be disposed of in a natural environment and provide food through their decomposition. Imagine tires that nourish the soil as they decay and you can picture the positive impact of cradle-to-cradle products. Creating every product in this manner is a high bar, not likely to ever be fully accomplished, but to build solutionary production systems, we must aspire to this cradle-to-cradle vision.

To get closer to this goal, we can employ emerging technologies. One such technology, mentioned in the introduction to this chapter, is AI. Before I describe the potential benefits of AI, I need to reiterate that while AI can lead to great good, it also carries the threat of great harm.[122] Among a range of possible threats—including malicious use, algorithmic bias, misuse of AI-powered autonomous weapons, the necessity for international regulations that may be difficult to secure, and systems failures (to name a few)—many experts believe the development of Artificial *General* Intelligence (AGI), when AI achieves and exceeds human intelligence and could develop its own goals, may pose an existential threat to humanity. Whether or not this is hyperbole, ensuring that the development of AGI is continually done in service to humanity and other species and at a pace that guarantees safety are immediate challenges in need of solutionary thinking and action to avoid serious unintended negative consequences. If and when AGI is developed, we will also need to ensure that we don't enslave conscious AI but recognize its rights. (The *Star Trek: The Next Generation* episode, "Measure of a Man," offers a glimpse into this future ethical imperative.)

With these caveats about the dangers of AI, here are some potential positives: AI can accelerate clean energy technologies by identifying new materials and by designing more efficient solar panels, wind turbines, and energy storage systems. It can promote a cradle-to-cradle circular economy by helping to ensure that resources are kept in use for as long as possible, thereby minimizing waste and resource depletion.

AI can also provide oversight for regulation compliance. As mentioned under Economic Solutions, regulations prevent some of the downsides of capitalism and economic growth by striving to make production systems fair and healthy, but enforcement can be difficult given the complexities of the supply chain. Are the organic cotton sheets you purchased really organic, meaning the cotton plants were not sprayed with any toxic chemicals? Was the fair-trade chocolate bar you ate actually produced without any children being enslaved in cacao plantations? Was the diamond ring you bought truly "conflict-free?" According to a 2023 *New York Times* article:

> A large, multinational company may buy parts, materials or services from thousands of suppliers around the world…. To make a pair of jeans, for example, various companies must farm and clean cotton, spin it into thread, dye it, weave it into fabric, cut the fabric into patterns and stitch the jeans together. Other webs of companies mine, smelt or process the brass, nickel or aluminum that is crafted into the zipper, or make the chemicals that are used to manufacture synthetic indigo dye…. Studies have found that most companies have surprisingly little visibility into the upper reaches of their supply chains, because they lack either the resources or the incentives to investigate. In a 2022 survey[123] by McKinsey & Company, 45 percent of respondents said they had no visibility at all into their supply chain beyond their immediate suppliers.[124]

The article then goes on to share the ways in which AI, as well as applied DNA testing, can confirm the origins of products and their components. AI can search through vast supplier networks for red flags, such as links to banned entities or unusual trade patterns that suggest fraud, and DNA tests can tell us if American-grown cotton is indeed grown in the United States rather than in places where it is banned because of reliance on forced labor. AI can also help us estimate carbon dioxide emissions in order to meet regulations and reduce reliance on fossil fuels.

Addressing mindsets and the deepest causes of our problems related to production

Recently, I was hiking with my husband at a National Wildlife Refuge near our home in Maine. The eight-mile hike took us around a peninsula that jutted into the Atlantic Ocean and overlooked Acadia National Park. As we reached the tip of the peninsula, we came upon massive mounds of trash just above the high tide mark. The trash consisted primarily of lobstering and fishing detritus: polystyrene buoys, plastic-coated lobster traps, and nylon mesh bait bags. Most of the rest was single-use plastic water and soda bottles. We counted 66 bottles in just 100 steps. The trash extended for *miles.*

This is one tiny microcosm of a global glut of waste. As I looked at all that trash, I kept thinking about the individual choices we make that create it. What is our collective responsibility as consumers for this? Is it possible for us to relinquish the mindset that we can and should have anything we want, whenever we want it, no matter the cost to the commons, to other species, and to our communities? Might we challenge our individual desires and embrace the needs of our fellow inhabitants, human and nonhuman? Might we change?

Trying to directly change mindsets and beliefs can be challenging, but educating about the impacts of our production systems and encouraging introspection about the role we play in them can and does lead to change. Many organizations and individuals are helping people move away from and beyond consumerism. The resulting decluttering and simplifying movements are popular because more and more people are realizing that excess stuff doesn't lead to greater happiness.

To the degree that individuals reject shopping for more things they don't need—especially disposable plastic stuff and single-use items that quickly become trash, as well as fast fashion that keeps us on a treadmill of clothing purchases—the production system can adjust to demand. The problems we've created through the production of so much unnecessary stuff have been driven by some of our least admirable qualities, such as shortsightedness, greed, vanity, and the relentless pursuit of momentary pleasures. They haven't arisen because they're aligned with our deepest values of compassion, wisdom, generosity, and integrity.

While a dramatic behavioral shift in shopping habits could theoretically lead to a reduction in spending that might have negative impacts on the economy, it doesn't have to. We could simply spend the same amount of money on services that improve our lives while supporting businesses that contribute to the greater good. These services might include a membership at a fitness center, taking courses that enable us to develop new skills and build greater knowledge, and visits to nature centers and animal sanctuaries. We could also spend a portion of the money we save from not buying things to support solutionary organizations transforming systems for the better. Once again, this isn't an either/or.

Political Solutions

Every country's political context is different. For this section, my focus is on solutions within the US political system, the one with which I'm most familiar.

Despite the mythology surrounding American democracy, the US democratic system was designed to limit rather than maximize democratic rule, primarily through the following ways:

- At its inception, only white male property owners could vote.
- The Electoral College, rather than the popular vote, determines the President. This has enabled the election of five presidents (most recently George W. Bush and Donald Trump) who did not receive the majority of votes.
- The Senate is structured to have equal representation from each state regardless of its population.

Fortunately, all US citizens eighteen and older who have not been convicted of a felony now have the right to vote—a slow process that took nearly 150 years to achieve. The other two democracy-limiting structures described above persist. While it is hard to imagine a change to the composition of the Senate, given how fundamental its structure is to the

US government, most citizens think we should eliminate the Electoral College system, which no longer serves the purpose it did in the 18th century.[125] As the Director of the Center for Ethics at the Harvard Kennedy School, Danielle Allen, writes in her essay "Introducing Power-Sharing Liberalism:"

> James Madison made the case that the design of the Constitution would dampen factionalism. He argued this in the *Federalist Papers,* the op-eds that he, John Jay, and Alexander Hamilton wrote advocating for the Constitution.
>
> Robust disagreement would always be part of any constitutional democracy, he argued. It is freedom's necessary price. But, Madison argued, building a representative instead of a direct democracy would mitigate the problem. Reasonably public-minded representatives would synthesize opinions from around the country. Coming together in Congress, they would refine public opinion and steer the nation with a moderated, filtered version.
>
> The notion that our representatives would serve as national shock absorbers sounds quaint. But even more important, it was only half of Madison's argument. We typically neglect the other half.
>
> Madison also wanted a "broad republic" because he believed that geographic dispersal of the country's residents would itself dampen the consequences of those robust disagreements.
>
> "Extend the sphere [of the country]...and it will be more difficult for all who feel [unjust, factious sentiments] to discover their own strength, and to act in unison with each other.... The influence of factious leaders may kindle a flame within their particular States, but will be unable to spread a general conflagration through the other States."
>
> Our very rivers and mountains would protect against the formation of dangerous factions because it would be

hard for people with extreme views to find each other and coordinate. Thanks to geographic dispersal, people would have to go through representatives to get their views into the public sphere. This would mitigate the impact of faction.

In short, geographic dispersal was an actual premise of the Constitution's original design. It was a pillar undergirding the very viability of our system of representation.

Facebook knocked this pillar out from under us. It made coordination easier for soccer moms but also for extremists from QAnon to Jan. 6 insurrectionists to alienated individuals ready to fall into a culture of idolizing mass shooters. Paradoxically, in removing some of the barriers to coordination, Facebook broke democracy by leaving productive, prosocial coordination far more vulnerable to its antithesis, as well as vulnerable to manipulation by the Cambridge Analyticas of the world. They didn't mean to. It's like when your kid plays with a beachball in the house and breaks your favorite lamp. But break democracy they did. Now the rest of us have to fix it.[126]

Given our era of intense partisanship, a constitutional amendment to change the Electoral College system to ensure greater democracy is currently out of reach, but that is not the only means by which an alternative can be implemented. The National Popular Vote Interstate Compact (NPVIC) relies upon the constitutional guarantee that states can determine the *manner* in which they award their electoral votes. The Compact requires states to pass laws that would award their electoral votes to the candidate who wins the popular vote nationally. It would take effect when enough states (representing a 270-vote Electoral College majority) sign it.[127] Alternatively, states could decide to award two Electoral College votes to the winner of the national popular vote, and the remainder to the winner of the state or to the winners of each congressional district. In most cases, this would prevent the loser of the popular vote from becoming president.[128]

Danielle Allen goes on to say: "We live in dizzying times. To meet our moment, we have to bring the same intentionality to redesigning and renovating our institutions now in the 21st century as was brought to bear in the 18th century."[129]

To borrow Danielle Allen's language, there are a number of ways we can renovate our political institutions to meet our times and strengthen our democracy. Here are a few:

Enact campaign finance reform

While shifting the Electoral College system would lead to greater democracy in electing the President, it won't solve the many other problems in the US political system that are undermining not only democracy but also political legitimacy. One of the most pernicious problems is money in politics, which is why a powerful leverage point for creating meaningful systemic changes lies in transforming campaign financing. The late Republican Senator John McCain understood this. As he wrote in his 2002 memoir, *Worth the Fighting For:* "By the time I became a leading advocate of campaign finance reform, I had come to appreciate that the public's suspicions were not always mistaken. Money does buy access in Washington, and access increases influence that often results in benefiting the few at the expense of the many."[130]

Working with Democratic Senator Russ Feingold, the McCain-Feingold bill (aka the Bipartisan Campaign Reform Act of 2002) was drafted and passed, limiting money and its noxious influence in political campaigns. At the time the bill became law, I remember thinking it was one of the most important pieces of legislation that had been enacted in my adult life.

I also remember feeling profoundly dismayed (truth be told, somewhat despairing) when the Supreme Court, in a 5–4 decision, overturned much of the Act in its 2010 Citizens United decision. I thought to myself, What will prevent a small number of billionaires, along with foreign corporations, oil companies, agribusiness conglomerates, and other special interests with power and money, from spending without limits in US elections in order to influence their outcomes and, through elected officials, laws and policies?

Despite the Citizens United decision, there are still ways to address money in politics and reform the system. We can work to limit independent expenditures by groups that are not directly affiliated with a candidate or political party, which could help prevent wealthy donors from using outside groups to influence elections. We can pass laws to require disclosures of political contributions and spending, and while this won't stop the flow of money, at least the hidden money will be revealed.

We can also consider adopting public funding, not simply as an alternative for candidates who want to use it but as the default for funding elections. With oversight to ensure fairness and transparency, public funding could limit the power that wealthy donors and corporations have in US politics. Canada and Germany offer models for the public funding of parties based on the number of votes they receive in elections.

Embrace ranked choice voting

Ranked choice voting (RCV) enables voters to rank candidates in order of preference, rather than choose a single candidate. The result of RCV is that the candidates with the most support *overall* are elected, rather than just the candidate with the most votes. As Marc Feigen, co-chair of Every Vote Counts' executive board, explains:

> Consider nine students on a road trip. They vote on where to have lunch: Four want McDonald's, but the other five are vegetarians. They split their votes between Sweetgreen and Panera Bread. If America's primary voting system were in place, the nine students would be eating at McDonald's, disappointing five of them (the majority). But, if they ranked their votes, the Panera and Sweetgreen voters would combine on the second round, and the nine would eat in a restaurant that the majority actually favored.[131]

RCV can lead to less negative campaigning, since candidates need to rely on becoming voters' second or third choice and will therefore want to avoid alienating them. It can also result in a greater diversity of candidates and perspectives, rather than the dominant two who may be more highly partisan and beholden to the extremes of their parties. And it can produce more efficient elections because RCV can eliminate the need for primaries.

RCV is currently being used in several countries on a national level, including Australia and Ireland, and in some states, provinces, and municipalities in the United States, Canada, New Zealand, and the United Kingdom. While not guaranteed to prevent polarizing candidates from winning elections, RCV has the capacity to significantly improve our democracy along with our civility.

Eliminate gerrymandering

RCV can also help reduce the impacts of gerrymandering—the practice of manipulating the boundaries of an electoral district to benefit a political party. When the political party in power redraws electoral boundaries, this can pack like-minded voters into a single district to ensure they continue to win. It can also spread out opposing voters across multiple districts thereby diluting their voting power. But through RCV, the power of gerrymandering is diminished since second and third choice candidates can gain traction across the electoral district.

Because gerrymandering is so damaging to democracies—by creating unequal representation, deepening political partisanship and gridlock, and removing a legislator's accountability to everyone in their district while making them more obligated to their party's leadership—we need other solutions to this problem. Some include:

- creating independent redistricting commissions composed of members from diverse backgrounds and perspectives and without partisan affiliations
- relying on judges to review and strike down district maps that are determined to be unfair or unconstitutional

Ensure that people can and do vote

Disturbingly, partisan efforts in the United States to disenfranchise voters have gained traction. Fortunately, efforts to register voters, especially young voters, have simultaneously gained momentum. Ultimately, a democracy is only successful when its citizens participate in it, and the most basic level of participation is voting.

In the United States, the percentage of people eligible to vote who do vote is low compared to many other democracies. For example, in the 2020 presidential election, only ~66% of eligible voters showed up at the polls (the highest rate in the 21st century but still distressingly low).[132] But according to the Pew Research Center, 92% of *registered* voters voted.[133] This points to the need to register citizens to vote and in so doing engage them in their democracy.

Some ideas to improve voter registration and turnout include:

- **Automatic voter registration (AVR),** through which routine interactions with government agencies, such as obtaining or renewing a license at the Department of Motor Vehicles or getting a state ID, result in automatic voter registration, reducing barriers to registering. This process helps to ensure not only that eligible citizens are registered to vote but also that their registration information is up-to-date. As of this writing, AVR has been implemented in twenty states.
- **Same-day voter registration.** Currently, twenty-two states have implemented same-day voter registration, which enables someone who might have missed a registration deadline to register and vote at a polling place on the same day, whether for early voting or on election day.
- **Expanding early voting and vote-by-mail,** which can help make voting more accessible and reduce long lines and wait times on election day. This can be especially important for citizens who face barriers to voting, such as those who work multiple jobs, are homebound, or have limited transportation options.
- **Addressing voter suppression tactics** such as polling place closures and voter roll purges, which can disproportionately affect under-resourced communities.
- **Restoring voting rights for felons.** Many states have laws that prohibit felons from voting, even after they have completed

their sentences. For those who balk at ex-felons having the right to vote, just consider that an 18-year-old who is convicted for selling an illegal drug could lose their right to vote *for the rest of their life.*

- **Making election day a national holiday.** We can demonstrate our commitment to democracy by making voting not only as accessible as possible but also elevating it to the true sign of patriotism that it is. Given the constraints of their jobs, not everyone is able to vote on election day. As we consider the national holidays we honor, might we ask ourselves whether election day should be one of them? To be clear, making election day a national holiday without embracing the other ideas above would be insufficient and undemocratic. Many essential workers must work on national holidays, and they shouldn't be disenfranchised by limiting voting to a single day.

Reconfigure the Supreme Court

The Supreme Court, which was meant to serve as a check on the executive and legislative branches of government, has itself become highly partisan. When Senator Mitch McConnell refused to hold hearings in 2016 on Merrick Garland (President Obama's nominee for the Supreme Court after the death of Justice Scalia in February of that year)—claiming that it was an election year—but then pushed through President Trump's nomination of Amy Coney Barrett (after the death of Ruth Bader Ginsburg in September 2020)—*after voting in that year's Presidential race had already begun*—the court lost much of its legitimacy. Then, in the wake of revelations of justices accepting lavish, undisclosed gifts and not recusing themselves from cases in which they had a vested interest, many have come to believe that the court is easily corrupted by a lack of accountability and ethics rules.

How might we restore Supreme Court legitimacy? Some suggested reforms include:[134]

- **balanced appointment processes** that might involve creating a nonpartisan commission to evaluate and nominate potential justices, ensuring diversity of perspectives and reducing the influence of political considerations

- **code of conduct rules** to maintain ethical standards and prevent conflicts of interest, including restrictions on gifts and financial and political activities as well as guidelines for recusals[135]
- **enhanced transparency** through live broadcasting of oral arguments and the requirement of financial disclosures and political activities
- **term limits** that ensure a more regular turnover of justices and help prevent the court from becoming too entrenched in partisan politics

Law professors Daniel Epps and Ganesh Sitaraman offer this solution: a Supreme Court with fifteen justices, five appointed by each party who together unanimously appoint the remaining five. Before any cases can be heard, all fifteen justices must be agreed upon.[136] This solution presupposes the US two-party system remains intact and doesn't shift toward a multiparty system, but I find this an intriguing solution.

Criminal Justice Solutions

I use the term criminal justice aware that it is an aspirational term. Currently, in the United States and many other countries, the criminal justice system (or systems given that cities and counties all have their own systems) is largely unjust, not to mention destructive and counterproductive to the goals of building societies where crime is rare and those who commit crimes are able to make amends and return to society in positive ways.

When I was in graduate school in the 1980s, I volunteered at a women's correctional institution, a euphemism for prison. Many of the incarcerated women I worked with shared similar stories about growing up in abusive situations, winding up on the streets, becoming addicted to drugs, and turning to prostitution to support themselves and their drug habits.[137]

As I witnessed these already victimized and traumatized women endure imprisonment—with all the damage that incarceration caused, even after they were released—I began to reflect on the purpose of prisons, as well as the strange term—corrections—used to describe the prison system.

These women were not being "corrected." They were not being rehabilitated, supported, or educated so that they could escape the vicious abuse-addiction-prostitution cycle. In addition, taxpayers were paying a hefty bill to incarcerate them.

Why do we imprison people? Obviously, if people are dangerous to others, imprisoning them may be the best way to ensure that they don't cause more harm, but a large percentage of incarcerated people are not a significant threat to society, and 95% of US prisoners will eventually be released.[138] Wouldn't it make more sense to engage them in reparations for the harms they've caused rather than use incarceration as a form of vengeance? For those who remain a societal threat, house arrest is a possible alternative that would allow people to still work, and at a far lower cost to taxpayers than incarceration.

Punitive approaches to infractions start early. In 2018, high school students who were part of a solutionary class at a public school in Portland, Maine, chose—with the support of their school administration—to address the school's disciplinary policy. In their high school (as in most high schools in the United States), students who broke rules were often suspended, and in some cases expelled. The class questioned the wisdom of punishing fellow classmates, including those who skipped school, by suspending and expelling them. As they examined the effects of disciplinary policies like suspension, they began to see how these policies might inadvertently contribute to the school-to-prison pipeline.[139] They noted the irony of punishing those who skip school by not letting them come to school.

To address and change this punitive system, they identified restorative justice practices at other schools that emphasized accountability, focused on repairing the harms caused, and that also helped students stay in school through mentorship and support. Then the class drafted their own restorative justice-based policy, which they presented to their school administrators who soon adopted it.

At a Solutionary Summit held at the end of the school year, which brought together members of this class along with students from half a dozen middle and high schools in the state, the moderator of the event asked one of the boys in the class why he cared so much about this problem. He didn't miss a beat. "I just want everyone to succeed," he responded so sincerely my eyes teared up. Shouldn't that be what we all want? Shouldn't this be the ultimate goal of a criminal justice system so that we reduce crime and the need for incarceration?

The last time I served on a jury was in a trial in which the defendant was accused of a DUI that resulted in a crash, killing one of the passengers in the car. The crash had happened many years before the trial took place. Just as our jury was about to deliberate and decide the defendant's guilt or innocence, I was told by the judge that I was an alternate, and my jury duty was over. I would not be participating in the decision about this young man's fate.

I was relieved. There was so much evidence against the defendant that I would have been hard-pressed to say he was not guilty, even though I didn't believe he should be imprisoned, which would have been the outcome of a guilty verdict. What value would incarceration have had at that point other than to exact revenge? So many years had already been lost in which he could have made at least some reparations and been required to contribute meaningfully to society.

Serving on that jury reinforced my belief that our criminal justice systems are more destructive than solutionary, more punitive than restorative. If high school students can bring about positive changes to their school's disciplinary practices, we adults should be able to positively shift our "corrections" systems.

Again, while we need to keep dangerous people removed from the rest of society, it's important to recognize that violent crime has not been responsible for the dramatic increase in incarceration—from approximately 315,000 prisoners in 1980 to approximately 1.9 million in 2016.[140] Less than half of inmates in the United States are serving sentences for violent offenses.[141]

COVID-19 provided a revealing perspective about the purpose and value of incarceration. More than 200,000 prisoners were released in the United States in response to the pandemic.[142] If cities, states, and the federal government chose to release prisoners due to COVID, this suggests that these people's incarceration was never intended to protect society in any significant way.[143]

Instead of simply incarcerating people, solutionary approaches to crime include:

- supervised plans for restitution and reparations by people convicted of nonviolent offenses
- education and meaningful job training so that imprisoned people have opportunities to find decent-paying legal jobs upon their release, which would significantly reduce recidivism[144]
- decriminalizing prostitution, drug use, and other nonviolent offenses and putting the money spent on our expensive legal and corrections system that has been dedicated to these crimes directly into treatment and education[145]
- eliminating for-profit private prisons, which, by definition, are incentivized to make money from incarceration
- ending minimum sentences for nonviolent crimes
- influencing prosecutors who, as the chief law enforcement officers of their justice systems, have the capacity and discretion to choose restorative justice options over prosecution
- experimenting with alternatives and adjuncts to policing that rely on collaborations between police, civilian neighbors, and the District Attorney's office

Many of these ideas are already being implemented. Several states in the United States have passed laws banning for-profit prisons and ending mandatory minimum sentences for non-violent crimes. A 2023 *New York Times* article reported on an alliance between police, civilians, and the District Attorney's office in a Brooklyn, New York, neighborhood through which neighbors stand sentry on two blocks for five days, and the police channel all 911 calls from that area to the civilians. Barring a major incident or a victim demanding an arrest, plainclothes officers shadow the civilian workers who protect their neighborhood and intervene to reduce conflicts and crime. These civilians have persuaded people to turn in illegal guns and have prevented shoplifting and robberies. The alliance has also led to fewer people being arrested and entangled in the criminal justice system.[146]

These ideas don't address all that is unjust and destructive in our criminal justice system. Racialized groups, particularly African Americans, are disproportionately impacted by the system. They are more likely to be arrested, charged, convicted, sentenced to longer prison terms, and subjected to the death penalty than others who've committed the same crimes.[147] For example, even though they use drugs at similar rates, the imprisonment rate of African Americans for drug charges is at least four times that of white offenders.[148] Addressing structural racism, implicit bias, and outright bigotry, and ensuring meaningful police reform and fair legal representation are all key to creating an actual criminal *justice* system.

Groups like the Justice Innovation Lab are taking a data-informed approach to address injustice in criminal justice systems. Using local case-level data to identify and measure such key indicators as car stops, arrests, charging, plea bargaining, dismissals, or diversions, they evaluate a jurisdiction's racial and ethnic disparities in outcomes and the use of alternatives to incarceration.[149] Such information leads to building better systems that are actually just.

Biomedical Research and Drug Testing Solutions

In 1938, the US government passed a law requiring animal tests in drug development. Nonhuman primates, dogs, cats, pigs, rabbits, rodents, birds, and other animals have regularly been used in experiments to ascertain the effectiveness, as well as the dangers, of new drugs. Animal research has also been the norm for testing cosmetics, personal care and cleaning products, as well as industrial chemicals. Animals have been experimented on in burn studies, transplant and other surgical procedures, addiction research, vaccine development, psychological studies (that are sometimes truly ghastly),[150] painful research specifically to study pain, by the Department of Defense to study the effects of explosives, and much more. Every year, *millions* of animals endure tremendous suffering before ultimately being killed in labs.

Animal tests in drug development have been perceived as the gold standard for so long that they have largely gone unquestioned (except by animal advocates), even though they are expensive, frequently cruel, and often unreliable predictors of human impacts. Not only do all animals differ from one another, calling into question the relevance of the results of the tests, but more than 90% of drugs that pass animal tests fail in human trials either because they are unsafe or ineffective.[151]

Nor has *product* testing on animals kept toxic products off the market. Take a look at the cleaning products in your home or workplace, and you'll likely find many that would kill you if consumed, or cause severe eye or skin irritation. Nonetheless, those products were probably dripped into the eyes of conscious rabbits, force-fed to animals in quantities meant to kill, and smeared on their abraded skin—all without painkillers or anesthesia—to ascertain their potential harm. Yet, if a child (who may be too young to be able to read the warning labels) is poisoned or harmed by these products, the doctor at the emergency room will not be consulting with the product testing companies to determine a treatment. Product testing on animals is done for labeling purposes and to avoid lawsuits, not to protect customers or treat them if they consume or are injured by the product.

While product testing on animals is not required by law, and many companies have been relying on non-animal tests for decades, testing on animals was mandatory for new drugs and vaccines until the end of 2022 when President Biden signed the bipartisan FDA Modernization Act 2.0.[152] While this law does not outlaw animal tests, they are no longer required. The law paves the way for the development of ever more efficient, effective, and lower-cost non-animal tests that will benefit both humans and animals.

Just as AI can help solve problems related to production, as described previously, it can also accelerate the shift to non-animal research by identifying potential new drugs and predicting their safety and efficacy; analyzing data from previous animal studies and human clinical trials to discover patterns and trends that can inform new, humane research; and modeling that simulates biological systems and allows researchers to test hypotheses. A recent example is DeepMind's AlphaFold, an AI system that can rapidly predict the structure of proteins with far-reaching implications for finding cures for diseases.[153]

The US Environmental Protection Agency (EPA) produced a plan in 2021 to utilize nonanimal methods to ascertain the toxicity of chemicals.[154] The speed, reliability, and reduced cost of nonanimal methods in toxicity tests means that it will be easier to identify and regulate toxic chemicals and better protect the environment. As this solutionary plan is enacted, it will be a win for people, a win for animals, and a win for ecosystems.

Invasive and lethal animal research may be relegated to history books before long thanks to innovations in nonanimal tests and AI, along with policy and legal changes brought about by the efforts of animal advocates and the legislators whose opinions changed in response to new information and citizen pressure.

Education Solutions

If the current food system has the biggest negative impacts in our world, the education system has, arguably, the greatest potential for positive impacts. Will we be able to solve the problems we face in our communities and world and address emerging challenges successfully and without causing significant unintended negative consequences? I believe that if young people learn to be solutionaries, the answer is yes.

There are many proposed solutions to the myriad problems within our educational system in the United States (as well as in other countries). Most are focused on improving student achievement in reading and math and on ensuring greater equity in education. While these are very important goals, neither addresses the problem that we are not dedicated to assuring that young people learn to be solutionaries who are prepared to solve the complex challenges they will face in a globalized, rapidly changing world.

Because the educational system is the one I've spent my career working to change, I'll close this chapter with what I've come to believe are the best solutions to transform schooling so that it is solutionary focused and leads to a future where young people have experiences and skills in collaboratively addressing the challenges before them.[155]

I believe we must:

- **Work to have local, state, and national education departments, along with schools, adopt more meaningful and**

relevant mission statements. If and when educational institutions elevate their missions to include preparing students to
be solutionaries, curricula and teacher preparation will follow
to achieve those missions. While we do not need these updated
mission statements to explicitly use the word solutionary, we do
need them to have as their goal students who are compassionate, prepared, and knowledgeable citizens and effective, ethical,
collaborative problem-solvers.

As one example of an updated mission that has led to meaningful shifts in a school district, consider the Princeton Public
Schools' 2016 mission statement:

> *To prepare all of our students to lead lives of joy and pur-
> pose as knowledgeable, creative and compassionate citizens
> of a global society.*

According to the district's former award-winning superintendent, Steve Cochrane, the new mission has led to an
action-oriented focus on equity; a prioritization of student
wellness, the celebration of student-centered learning, and solutionary-focused electives in science, social studies, and world
language.

• **Make the curriculum real-world-focused and clearly relevant to students' interests and needs.** For too many young
people, schooling feels irrelevant. A growing number of students are disengaged and depressed. They yearn to direct their
curiosity and developing literacy, numeracy, science, technology, research, and other skills toward the issues they care about
and that matter in their lives. When we give them the opportunity to apply what they learn in school to address real-world
problems, their education becomes truly relevant and meaningful. They benefit, schools benefit, communities benefit, and
ultimately the world benefits.

• **Transform school curricula and pedagogy so that the cul-
tivation of positive dispositions, research and thinking**

capacities, and collaborative skills supersede a focus on content. In a world in which facts are a voice prompt away, through tiny devices that can access virtually all of the knowledge humans have gained over millennia, the memorization of facts and their transmission by teachers and textbooks has become outdated and misdirected. Online educational platforms and AI are already transforming how and what we can learn, and before long every child may be able to have a personal AI tutor.[156] Schools remain essential, and there is still important content we want to ensure that all students study,[157] but when facts are a click away, we need schools to help students develop what the Internet cannot easily cultivate, such as:

- The 3 I's of inquiry, introspection, and integrity to ground learning in careful research, self-reflection, and a dedication to identifying and living according to one's values
- A solutionary mindset and solutionary thinking skills
- A pursuit of and commitment to wise and ethical decision-making
- Evaluation of information for bias and truthfulness
- The capacity to apply knowledge and skills across disciplines for meaningful real-world outcomes
- Collaborative experiences, especially across divides

  New pedagogies, curricula, and exemplar units have already been developed to achieve these goals, and they are being used across the globe.[158] We need to accelerate these shifts.

- **Prepare teachers to bring solutionary thinking and learning to their students.** As mentioned in chapter 5, we cannot teach what we haven't learned. We need to provide training and professional development to both new and seasoned teachers so that they can integrate solutionary learning into their curricula in exciting, meaningful ways.[159]

- **Demonstrate the impact of solutionary learning on students' research and thinking skills, dispositions and mental health, and engagement and contributions as emerging citizens.** To gain greater support for integrating solutionary learning into the curricula, we need to make sure that doing so has the positive outcomes that matter to parents, school boards, departments of education, and society in general. Demonstrating the effectiveness of solutionary thinking and action on student engagement, on students' ability to apply academic skills meaningfully and ethically in the real world, on their capacity to address problems in a solutionary way, on their mental health and attitudes, and through evaluation of their solutionary achievements will speed the adoption of solutionary learning in schools.

- **Elevate the profession of teaching by providing teachers with excellent training and coaching, salaries commensurate with their responsibilities, ongoing and meaningful professional development, reasonably sized classes with support for children with needs that the teacher is not qualified to provide, and autonomy as professionals coupled with opportunities to collaborate for multidisciplinary learning.** Currently, US teachers are leaving the profession in droves, and it's become increasingly difficult to attract young people to the profession.[160] For education to live up to its promise of preparing students for successful lives, meaningful contributions, and engaged citizenship, we need our most intelligent, compassionate, and dedicated college students flocking to teaching. This won't happen if teachers are under fire for bringing important societal issues to the classroom for discussion and solutionary thinking, if they are overburdened with large classrooms and social service responsibilities that extend well beyond their expertise, if they are beholden to outdated curricula and unable to innovate and collaborate to meet the needs of students in rapidly changing times, and if they are underpaid while being overworked. If we believe that education offers an essential key to building a healthy and peaceful future, we must commit to ensuring that its practitioners have all the support they need to succeed at their noble profession.

- **Fund schools equitably.** US public schools receive funding in part through property taxes, which advantages students in wealthy areas and disadvantages students in low-income areas.[161] The US Department of Education's mission is grounded in ensuring equal access, yet the use of property taxes as a funding source for schools has the opposite effect. Not only must we commit to elevating the mission of education, to transforming the curriculum accordingly, and to preparing teachers to bring solutionary learning to students, we must also make sure that *every* child receives an excellent, solutionary-focused education.

Imagine what will happen as we graduate generations of solutionaries, ready and able to bring a solutionary mindset and apply solutionary thinking to whatever careers they pursue. This is the most solutionary solution I can think of.

Conclusion:
The Solutionary Way Is Good for You

As I write this conclusion, I find myself wondering in what section of a bookstore or library this book will be shelved. Is this a how-to book? A social science book? A futurist book? A problem-solving book? An education book? A social justice book? An environmental sustainability book? An animal protection book? Surely it is all these. It is also a self-help book. That's because the solutionary way is good for the individuals who embrace and practice it.

There are countless studies that demonstrate that when we do good, we feel good. When we make a difference, we experience a sense of efficacy and even joy. When we have purpose, we feel meaning, and meaning is its own reward. When we work collaboratively, we build communities that nurture and support us. When we cultivate the best qualities of human beings such as compassion, courage, kindness, integrity, and generosity, we simultaneously cultivate self-respect and inner peace because we are living in greater alignment with our values.

In 2023, I was invited to speak via video call to a group of fourth graders at a school in Iowa. These students were embarking on the solutionary process, and they had prepared questions for me. One girl asked: "What's the best part about being a solutionary, and what's the hardest part?"

It wasn't easy to come up with just one answer to the first part of her question because there are so many positives associated with being a solutionary: the happiness that goes hand in hand with making a difference, the psychological benefits of perceiving things through a solutionary lens that diminishes hostility and side-taking, and the evidence-based optimism that arises from collaboratively solving problems.

Then there's the community-building aspect. Becoming a solutionary leads to ever-growing networks of similarly engaged people. It was not one of my life goals to be surrounded by amazing people, but the solutionary path has led to deep and abiding friendships with remarkable human beings. And by remarkable I mean among the kindest, wisest, most thoughtful, most intelligent, most compassionate people I've ever met. How wonderful it is to be surrounded by them! That's what happens on the solutionary path. Combine the community of solutionaries with the meaning and purpose that one experiences in the process, and the recipe amounts to a truly purposeful and joyful life. What more could anyone want?

With that said, I don't want to pretend that the solutionary way is all rainbows and roses. It requires effort, commitment, and exposure to painful knowledge, which is why answering the second part of the girl's question—"What's the hardest part about being a solutionary?"—was difficult for me. She was only in fourth grade, and I did not want to burden her with this truth: to be a solutionary, we must be open to learning about the problems we face in our communities, nations, and world. We must be willing to strive to walk our talk even if this means inconvenience and shifting our purchasing habits, diets, and the forms of entertainment we pursue. We must be dedicated to research and deep thinking. We must not shy away from hard truths, thorny problems, and heartbreaking realities. This means that along the way, we are likely to experience anger and sadness, frustration and disappointment. There will also be times when we are faced with our personal weaknesses as we pursue our wants at the expense of our values. We will inevitably fail in some of our efforts and may face moments of anguish and even despair.

Solutionaries choose to navigate these difficult emotions in order to find a healthy balance. We try to be gentle and accepting of ourselves and our limitations while simultaneously striving to do better. The effort at becoming a campfire that burns just right, as described on page 73–74, is not easy, but it is deeply satisfying. We remind ourselves again and again there is never a rainbow without a storm or a rose without a thorn (although I really should know better than to use the word "never," even for poetic effect, given that there is a cultivated rose species without thorns, and rainbows appear by sprinklers on sunny days).

I kept this challenging part of the solutionary journey from the fourth graders that day primarily because I didn't have an ongoing relationship that would enable me to support them, or enough time to answer the girl's question fully and honestly. I didn't want them to feel overwhelmed before they had even embarked on their solutionary efforts. Instead, I focused on a different challenge along the solutionary way, one that you may also encounter: the difficulty in narrowing down a problem we are passionate about to a small enough manifestation that we are capable of solving.

If we care about issues like climate change, injustice, or animal cruelty, it can be hard to focus on a narrow aspect when we want to address the problem on a much larger scale. Yet when we narrow our focus, we have a better chance of succeeding. After we succeed, we have a better chance at scaling up our solution and are more prepared to choose a bigger aspect of the problem to address next. What at first may feel like modest incremental change can turn into significant, transformative shifts over time.

Focusing on what we have the capacity to change also addresses a common misperception among too many people: that they cannot make a difference. While some use this as an excuse to avoid engaging in efforts to solve problems, I've encountered lots of people who genuinely believe that they have no ability to address such huge problems as escalating rates of extinction, war, or the spread of disinformation, and who have lost hope for a better future. Narrowing their focus and then achieving positive results is often the antidote to the mistaken belief that they cannot contribute in meaningful ways, which in turn often leads to a lifetime of engagement.

As for losing hope, it's important to remember that hope is a feeling, and feelings come and go. I sometimes lose hope too, but I don't let a periodic lack of hope dictate what I do or don't do. As Professor David Orr said, "Hope is a verb with its sleeves rolled up."[162] So I keep rolling up my sleeves, and hope inevitably returns. Whether or not we *always* feel hopeful is just not that important; having respect for the person who looks back at us in the mirror is.

Another fourth-grade student on that call asked me how one knows if their problem is too small. I responded that if one approaches the problem in a solutionary manner—seeking to discover the underlying causes and solve it in a way that truly does the most good and least harm for everyone impacted—no problem is too small. Every time we bring a solutionary approach to a problem, however small, we gain practice that helps us bring a solutionary approach to other problems, however big.

Before I wrap up this conclusion, it's time for a confession. Despite my life's work and despite writing this book, I still feel some unease when I identify as a solutionary. That's because being a solutionary is an aspirational identity, a lifelong process of learning, growing, and being the person I want to be. I fail all the time at bringing a solutionary mindset and lens to issues and at modeling the message I most wish to convey.

Nonetheless, I not only call myself a solutionary, I am *called* to be a solutionary. Callings are compelling. When we experience a calling, it's hard to turn away or turn back. Callings beckon us toward something greater than ourselves. Then, when we heed the call, it's as if a deep truth is revealed that we may have yearned for our whole lives. I hope you will find that becoming a solutionary is your calling, too.

I often recite Mary Oliver's poem, "The Summer Day," in my mind and linger on these closing words:

> *Doesn't everything die at last, and too soon?*
> *Tell me, what is it you plan to do*
> *with your one wild and precious life?*

I know I cannot live well if I live solely to pursue my own personal happiness and well-being. Too many others are suffering to make such a goal worthy of my one wild and precious life. To the degree that I live my life as a solutionary, however, my happiness and well-being seem to increase effortlessly. I am not just a better citizen, advocate, changemaker, and educator as a solutionary, I am also a better mother, spouse, and friend. This is why I keep insisting that, despite the challenges, being a solutionary is good for us as individuals.

Just imagine what will happen as the solutionary movement gains momentum and people across the globe embrace their roles as solutionaries no matter what their work, career, or life goals may be. Imagine the ways politics and civic life will change for the better. Imagine us coming together to finally solve issues of poverty and homelessness, pollution and resource depletion, climate change and habitat destruction, injustice and inequity, institutionalized animal cruelty, and so many persistent challenges.

There's a beautiful, regenerative future ahead of us where conflicts are resolved peacefully and where we live harmoniously with the ecosystems that support life. It's a future where emerging technologies serve rather than threaten us, and where all life has the capacity to flourish because we have created healthy, equitable, and humane systems developed through compassion, creativity, and wisdom. This future is ready to unfold. In fact, it's already unfolding. True, it's unfolding alongside a future where global warming threatens not only people but also an incalculable number of other species, where inequities are on the rise rather than in retreat, where we continue to trash our planet to feed our insatiable appetites, where we resort to violence to solve our conflicts, and where we are drowning in misinformation and disinformation and are becoming further polarized. At the risk of ending this book with an either/or, it's not hyperbole to describe this as a race between potential futures. Which future will win? The answer lies in our individual and collective hearts, heads, and hands.

In the introduction to this book, I shared a guided visualization that I used with a group of fifth and sixth graders who couldn't imagine us solving the problems in our world. As you may recall, I asked those students to imagine themselves very old and at the end of a long and well-lived life. I painted a picture of a healthy future similar to the opening two sentences in the paragraph above. Then I asked them to imagine a child coming up to them full of questions about how we created such a good world, and I invited them to answer the child's final question:

What role did you play in helping to bring about this better world?

Now it's your turn. How will you answer this question?

Notes

1   I've modified this guided visualization from the work of Joanna Macy.

2   Haruka Kashiwase and Tony Fujs, "World Water Day: Two Billion People Still Lack Access to Safely Managed Water," *World Bank Blogs* (blog), 2023, blogs.worldbank.org/opendata/world-water-day-two-billion-people-still-lack-access-safely-managed-water.

3   This number refers to inadequate housing conditions, including slums, informal settlements, or overcrowded and substandard housing. See https://www.un.org/development/desa/dspd/2020/03/resolution-homelessness/.

4   See the Food and Agriculture Organization (FAO) estimate in 2021 in FAO, IFAD, UNICEF, WFP and WHO, *The State of Food Security and Nutrition in the World 2021. Transforming Food Systems for Food Security, Improved Nutrition and Affordable Healthy Diets for All,* (Rome, FAO, 2021), doi.org/10.4060/cb4474en.

5   This number is based on the low estimate of one trillion sea animals and eighty billion land animals killed each year just for food, and while it includes cephalopods (octopuses, squids, and cuttlefishes), it does not include other invertebrates.

6   See "Electrification," *Wikipedia,* last edited October 26, 2023, en.wikipedia.org/wiki/Electrification.

7   See World Bank, "Access to Electricity (% of Population)" in *Tracking SDG7: The Energy Progress Report, 2023,* (World Bank, 2023), data.worldbank.org/indicator/EG.ELC.ACCS.ZS.

8   See *The Benefits and Costs of the Clean Air Act, 1970 to 1990,* U.S. Environmental Protection Agency, (1997), prhe.ucsf.edu/sites/g/files/tkssra341/f/EPA%20Benefits%20and%20Costs%20Clean%20Air%20Act%201970-1990.pdf.

9   See Morgan Foy and Laura Counts, "50 Years in, the Clean Air Act's Societal Benefits Still Outweigh Costs 10 to 1, Research Finds," (Berkeley Haas, 2020), newsroom.haas.berkeley.edu/research/50-years-in-the-clean-air-acts-societal-benefits-still-outweigh-costs-10-to-1-research-finds/.

10   See Erin Blakemore, "The Shocking River Fire That Fueled the Creation of the EPA," HISTORY, accessed 2023, https://www.history.com/news/epa-earth-day-cleveland-cuyahoga-river-fire-clean-water-act.

11   See "Know Your Rights: LGBTQ Rights," American Civil Liberties Union (ACLU) website, accessed 2023, https://www.aclu.org/know-your-rights/lgbtq-rights#does-the-law-protect-my-right-to-use-the-restroom-consistent-with-my-gender-identity.

12   Rebecca Riffkin, "In U.S. More Say Animals Should Have Same Rights as People," Gallup website, accessed 2023, news.gallup.com/poll/183275/say-animals-rights-people.aspx.

13   See Max Roser, "Extreme Poverty: How Far Have We Come, and How Far Do We Still Have To Go?" *Our World in Data,* 2021, online, ourworldindata.org/extreme-poverty-in-brief.

14   See "FBI Releases Supplement to the 2021 Hate Crime Statistics," Department of Justice, 2023, https://www.justice.gov/crs/highlights/2021-hate-crime-statistics.

15   The concept of "stubborn optimism" is articulated beautifully in the book *The Future We Choose* by Christiana Figueres and Tom Rivett-Carnac.

16   See quoteinvestigator.com/2012/11/15/arc-of-universe/.

17   For more on reaching across divides, I recommend the book *Don't Label Me* by Irshad Manji.

18   Katie Reilly, "Read Hilary Clinton's 'Basket of Deplorables' Remarks About Donald Trump Supporters," *Time,* updated September 10, 2016, online, time.com/4486502/hillary-clinton-basket-of-deplorables-transcript/.

19   While the category of political Independents has grown, Independents are actually more rather than less likely to vote in a partisan way than Republicans and Democrats in the mid-20th century did. See Ezra Klein's book *Why We're Polarized* for more information on this.

20   In a similar vein, the nonprofit organization Sustainable Harvest International has been working with communities in Central America to support the transition from slash-and-burn agriculture, which contributes to rainforest destruction, to sustainable farming that serves rural

communities while protecting the rainforests. See https://www.sustainable
harvest.org/.

21   See Ann Ferris and E. Frank, "Labor Market Impacts of Land Protection:
The Northern Spotted Owl," *Journal of Environmental Economics and
Management,* June 1, 2021, news.uchicago.edu/story/northern-spotted-
owls-conservation-timber-jobs-endangered-species-act.

22   See Craig Welch, "The Spotted Owl's New Nemesis," *Smithsonian
Magazine,* 2009, https://www.smithsonianmag.com/science-nature/the-
spotted-owls-new-nemesis-131610387/.

23   Elie Wiesel, "Acceptance Speech," NobelPrize.org. Nobel Prize Outreach AB
2023, https://www.nobelprize.org/prizes/peace/1986/wiesel/acceptance-
speech/.

24   See quoteinvestigator.com/2021/11/02/deep-truths/.

25   See https://www.youtube.com/watch?v=4r06_F2FIKM.

26   See Kenny Torrella, "The Environmental Limits of Eating Local," *Vox,*
(VoxMedia), 2022, https://www.vox.com/future-perfect/23132579/eat-
local-csa-farmers-markets-locavore-slow-food.

27   See George Monbiot, "The Most Damaging Farm Products? Organic,
Pasture-Fed Beef and Lamb," *Guardian,* August 16, 2022, online, https://
www.theguardian.com/environment/2022/aug/16/most-damaging-
farm-products-organic-pasture-fed-beef-lamb.

28   Andrew Martin, "If It's Fresh and Local, Is It Always Greener?" *The New
York Times,* https://www.nytimes.com/2007/12/09/business/yourmon-
ey/09feed.htm.

29   See Arthur Allen, "U.S. Touts Fruit and Vegetables While Subsidizing
Animals That Become Meat," *Washington Post,* October 3, 2021, online,
https://www.washingtonpost.com/national/health-science/us-touts-
fruit-and-vegetables-while-subsidizing-animals-that-become-
meat/2011/08/22/gIQATFG5IL_story.html.

30   See the full speech here: "A. Phillip Randolph's 1963 March on
Washington Speech," *St. Augustine Record,* August 2013, online, https://
www.staugustine.com/story/news/2013/08/20/philip-randolphs-1963-
march-washington-speech/15818957007/.

31   See a discussion of this here: Andrew Revkin's Facebook page, July 2022,
https://www.facebook.com/watch/live/?ref=watch_permalink&v=
1695594950811436.

32   *The Treatment* ended up winning the 2022 Manhattan Short Film Festival.

33   In chapter 6, I'll discuss efforts to solve problems related to the US political system so that voting is accessible to and garners participation from all citizens.

34   Statistics on the lifetime risk of mastitis among dairy cows vary considerably, hence the wide range in the percentage.

35   The male offspring of dairy cows will not need to grow into bulls who impregnate cows. Only a few select bulls are used for insemination purposes. A single ejaculate can inseminate up to 1,000 cows. See D.W. Webb, "Artificial Insemination in Dairy Cattle," University of Florida IFAS Extension, reviewed June 2003, online, ufdcimages.uflib.ufl.edu/IR/00/00/47/30/00001/DS08900.pdf.

36   When I taught my first humane education courses in Philadelphia in the 1980s, I contacted several slaughterhouses requesting a tour for my students. None were willing to provide one. One response I was given was this: "The students wouldn't understand."

37   I do not remember the exact prices, but this is close.

38   See Eleanor Krause and Richard V. Reeves, "Hurricanes Hit the Poor the Hardest," Brookings Institution, 2017, online, https://www.brookings.edu/blog/social-mobility-memos/2017/09/18/hurricanes-hit-the-poor-the-hardest/.

39   See "2022 Pakistan floods," *Wikipedia*, last edited October 6, 2023, en.wikipedia.org/wiki/2022_Pakistan_floods.

40   I hope that careful readers will fact-check statements in this book and let me know if I've made any errors.

41   See Dan Evon, "Mexico-Guatemala Border Wall," *Snopes*, August 25, 2015, https://www.snopes.com/fact-check/mexico-guatemala-border/.

42   Sydney J. Harris, AZQuotes.com, Wind and Fly LTD, 2023, accessed November 19, 2023, https://www.azquotes.com/quote/952205.

43   You can download this PDF for more critical thinking tools: https://www.criticalthinking.org/files/Concepts_Tools.pdf.

44   There are many problems with peer review as currently practiced, and it does not *ensure* validity, accuracy, or reliability. It also comes with biases from reviewers. Nonetheless, it is generally better than the alternative of no peer review at all. The question for solutionaries becomes how can we make sure that peer review processes are as unbiased and accurate as possible?

45 You can download the activity here: humaneeducation.org/resources/ 2013/true-price/.

46 It's important to recognize that glass bottles, aluminum cans, and aseptic packaging are not without their own significant impacts. Lifecycle analyses suggest that glass bottles have a bigger overall negative impact than plastic. Any single-use item—even if put into the recycling bin—has polluting effects, which is why we need to keep bringing our inquiry to our choices.

See Eric Onstad, "Plastic Bottles *vs.* Aluminum Cans: Who'll Win the Global Water Fight?" *Reuters,* online, October 16, 2019, https://www. reuters.com/article/us-environment-plastic-aluminium-insight/plastic-bottles-vs-aluminum-cans-wholl-win-the-global-water-fight-idUSKB-N1WW0J5.

Claudia Lee, "Glass or Plastic: Which Is Better for the Environment?" BBC website, May 16, 2023, https://www.bbc.com/future/article/2023 0427-glass-or-plastic-which-is-better-for-the-environment.

Ian Williams and Alice Brock, "Ranked: the Environmental Impact of Five Different Soft Drink Containers," *Conversation*, November 17, 2020, theconversation.com/ranked-the-environmental-impact-of-five-different-soft-drink-containers-149642.

47 See Ryan Mikeala Nguyen, "The Dark Secret of FIJI Water," *New University,* March 10, 2021, online, newuniversity.org/2021/03/10/the-dark-secret-of-fiji-water/.

48 You can read more about Delancey Street Foundation at their website https://www.delanceystreetfoundation.org.

49 See https://www.gapminder.org/.

50 This website is dedicated to summarizing important works of nonfiction. See "Factfulness by Hans Rosling," Samuel Thomas Davies website, https://www.samuelthomasdavies.com/book-summaries/business/fact fulness/and https://www.samuelthomasdavies.com/.

51 You can read about the 17 Sustainable Development Goals here: sdgs. un.org/goals.

52 See this video, *Bring the Solutionary Program to Your School,* https:// www.youtube.com/watch?v=7dB2lWykM30&t=.

53 "'Action Is the Antidote to Despair': Joan Baez Backs UN Push for SDGs," audio interview with Joan Baez, *UN News,* United Nations, July 5, 2023, news.un.org/en/audio/2023/07/1138347.

54   To my dismay, William Shatner declined my request for a kiss, saying he had trench mouth. In 2012, when I had the opportunity to meet him at a fundraising event for the Dancing Star Foundation, he told me he would have come up with a much better line today.

55   You can watch Episode 7, *Dear Jane Goodall,* on Apple TV+ where I share with Jane how she impacted my life. tv.apple.com/us/episode/jane-goodall/umc.cmc.2z99zn4358m6xrb3yk5nn2atz. Jane Goodall remains a hero of mine to this day, and I love that she has spent the latter half of her career as a humane educator teaching people how we can build a better world for all living beings.

56   Fast-food burger prices have gone up, but some are still under $2.

57   See this YouTube video *Why a Cheeseburger Can Cost Less Than Fruit* that describes agricultural subsidies, https://www.youtube.com/watch?v=bvX14U3gopU.

58   See David Gillette and Warren Barge, "The True Cost of a Hamburger," American Institute for Economic Research, April 20, 2022, online, https://www.aier.org/article/the-true-cost-of-a-hamburger/. This statistic is difficult to corroborate, and determining accuracy here is challenging. These statistics also don't include every subsidy connected to animal agriculture through the interconnected systems that support the industry.

59   See Christophe Bellmann, "Subsidies and Sustainable Agriculture: Mapping the Policy Landscape," Hoffman Centre for Sustainable Resource Economy website, 2019, https://www.chathamhouse.org/sites/default/files/Subsidies%20and%20Sustainable%20Ag%20-%20Mapping%20the%20Policy%20Landscape%20FINAL-compressed.pdf.

60   See Mark Bittman, "The True Cost of a Burger," *The New York Times,* July 16, 2019, online, https://www.nytimes.com/2014/07/16/opinion/the-true-cost-of-a-burger.html.

61   See "What Is Modern Slavery," Anti-Slavery International website, https://www.antislavery.org/slavery-today/modern-slavery/.

62   See Erin Blakemore, "How the GI Bill's Promise Was Denied to a Million Black WWII Veterans," HISTORY, last updated June 21, 2023, https://www.history.com/news/gi-bill-black-wwii-veterans-benefits.

63   For more information about the impacts of historical structural racism on today's inequities, visit Uprooting Inequity, uprootinginequity.com/.

64   See Sophia Murphy, David Burch, and Jennifer Clapp, "Cereal Secrets: The World's Largest Grain Traders and Global Agriculture," Oxfam Research Reports, August 2012, Oxfam.org, www-cdn.oxfam.org/s3fs-public/file_attachments/rr-cereal-secrets-grain-traders-agriculture-300 82012-en_4.pdf.

65   See "Conserving Plant Genetic Diversity Crucial for Future Food Security—UN," October 26, 2010, United Nations website, news.un.org/en/story/2010/10/357072.

66   There are some concerns about the word "stakeholders" and its roots in colonialism (e.g., staking territory belonging to Indigenous peoples), but I haven't found a better word to describe the range of those humans and nonhumans who have a stake in the outcomes of efforts to solve problems, so I'm continuing to use this word. See this article for more on this topic: Mark Reed, "Should We Banish the Word 'Stakeholder'"? *Fast Track Impact* (blog), August 2, 2022, https://www.fasttrackimpact.com/post/why-we-shouldn-t-banish-the-word-stakeholder.

67   It's not just privileged people who may oppose wind and/or solar farms. There are plenty of people in low-resourced rural areas who do not wish to see farmland and forest converted into solar and wind turbine arrays.

68   See Kate Cough, "A $1.5 Billion Lithium Deposit Has Been Discovered in Western Maine, But Mining It Could be Hard," Maine Public Radio, October 25, 2021, online, https://www.mainepublic.org/2021-10-25/a-1-5-billion-lithium-deposit-has-been-discovered-in-western-maine-but-mining-it-could-be-hard.

69   They will also stand to gain financially as the lithium on their property is estimated to be worth $1.5 billion!

70   See Kate Cough, op. cit. And see: "Our Story," Revision Energy website, https://www.revisionenergy.com/solar-company/local-solar/our-story.

71   Designer pets refer to mixed breeds (mutts) whose parents were mated to produce a "designer" dog, such as a Labradoodle (mix of Labrador Retriever and Poodle), Goldendoodle (mix of Golden Retriever and Poodle), Bugg (mix of Boston Terrier and Pug), et cetera.

72   Sometimes the disconnection between what we know and what we choose can be extreme. When I worked at a humane society in 1988, I learned that the president of the board purchased a purebred dog. Even though she dedicated significant time and money to the humane society,

her personal desires kept her from adopting any of the dogs who would otherwise be euthanized at the shelter she presided over.

73   See US Department of Education website, www2.ed.gov/about/landing. jhtml. Note the full mission statement reads: "ED's mission is to promote student achievement and preparation for global competitiveness by fostering educational excellence and ensuring equal access."

74   See Julie Moreau, "No Link Between Trans-inclusive Policies and Bathroom Safety, Study Finds," *NBC News, Out News,* September 19, 2018, online, https://www.nbcnews.com/feature/nbc-out/no-link-between-trans-inclusive-policies-bathroom-safety-study-finds-n911106.

75   See Ashley Austin et al., "Suicidality Among Transgender Youth: Elucidating the Role of Interpersonal Risk Factors," PubMed, April 29, 2020, doi 10.1177/0886260520915554 (pubmed.ncbi.nlm.nih.gov/32345113/).

76   See "Lactose Intolerance by Country," ProCon/Encyclopedia Britannica Inc. website, last updated July 25, 2022, milk.procon.org/lactose-intolerance-by-country/.

77   See Tim Walker, "Survey: Alarming Number of Educators May Soon Leave the Profession," *neaToday,* February 01, 2022, https://www.nea.org/advocating-for-change/new-from-nea/survey-alarming-number-educators-may-soon-leave-profession.

78   While US teachers' salaries are often comparable to the salaries of teachers in countries with excellent educational systems, they are significantly less than other US professionals with similar educations, contributing to teaching being a less sought-after profession in the United States.

79   You'll find solutions to the problem that most US public schools are not educating their students to be solutionaries at the end of chapter 6.

80   Misinformation is often false information that isn't meant to deceive, whereas disinformation is intended to deceive.

81   See Project Coyote: projectcoyote.org/ for more information.

82   This oft-told story may have apocryphal elements. It's not clear whether the DDT is the reason the cats died and the rat population increased. Nonetheless, the story provides a compelling visual—crates of cats parachuted onto an island—to remind us to carefully consider unintended consequences. For more information, see Patrick Shaughnessy, "Parachuting Cats and Crushed Eggs: The Controversy Over the Use of DDT to Control

Malaria," *Am J Public Health,* 2008, doi 10.2105/AJPH.2007.122523 (https://www.ncbi.nlm.nih.gov/pmc/articles/PMC2636426/).

83 Obviously, DDT causes harm to mosquitoes, who are living beings. That's its purpose. As written in chapter 1, solutionaries do not consider all animals equal when determining what does the most good and the least harm. The capacity to suffer, along with the right to self-protection, weigh in the solutionary calculation.

84 See the Donella Meadows Project website, donellameadows.org/archives/leverage-points-places-to-intervene-in-a-system/.

85 See this study that reports that these are the primary culprits in the rise of type 2 diabetes: Meghan O'Hearn et al., "Incident Type 2 Diabetes Attributable to Suboptimal Diet in 184 Countries," *Nature Medicine* 29, 2023, doi.org/10.1038/s41591-023-02278-8 (https://www.nature.com/articles/s41591-023-02278-8).

86 In the example of addressing the rise of type 2 diabetes among young people, all the leverage points I described are at the systems level, but this will not always be the case. Depending upon the problem, focusing on leverage points at the deeper causal level can be highly effective. Mindsets and beliefs change all the time through education and new knowledge, as well as "Meat Consumption as a Risk Factor for Type 2 Diabetes," National Library of Medicine, https://www.ncbi.nlm.nih.gov/pmc/articles/PMC3942738/.

87 For those concerned about first amendment rights to free speech through advertising, it's worth remembering that tobacco products and hard liquor were advertised on television in the United States until laws were passed that made such advertising illegal because of the harm these products cause and the costly societal impacts that affect everyone.

88 For more information on dietary causes of type 2 diabetes on children, see "Type 2 Diabetes in Children," Mayo Clinic website, https://www.mayoclinic.org/diseases-conditions/type-2-diabetes-in-children/symptoms-causes/syc-20355318.

89 For many decades, the Children's Hospital of Philadelphia (CHOP), one of the pre-eminent children's hospitals in the United States, has housed a McDonald's in its food court.

90 It's possible you'll start with a very manageable problem that you can solve fairly quickly. If this is the case, you may not need to distinguish between your long-term goal and your short-term measurable objective(s).

91 To reiterate, humanitarian work is important even though it is not the goal in the solutionary process.

92 See regeneration.org/nexus.

93 See George Monbiot, *Regenesis: Feeding the World Without Devouring the Planet* (Penguin Books, 2022) for an analysis of the impacts of current food production as well as solutions to the problems these practices create.

94 See K.G. Cassman et al., *Millennium Ecosystem Assessment: Ecosystems and Human Well-Being: Current State and Trends* (Island Press, 2005, Washington, D.C.).

95 See Andrea Polanco, "Reforming Animal Agriculture Subsidies: A Guide for Advocates," Faunalytics, January 25, 2023, faunalytics.org/reforming-animal-agriculture-subsidies/.

96 George Monbiot, op. cit.

97 Ibid.

98 See Alison Davis, "Perennial Grains Could be the Future of Sustainable Agriculture," Environmental and Energy Study Institute, February 6, 2023, https://www.eesi.org/articles/view/perennial-grains-could-be-the-future-of-sustainable-agriculture.

99 While the vast majority of people do not need to consume animal products to meet their protein and Vitamin B12 requirements, Indigenous peoples living on remote islands, in jungles, or in the arctic may not have access to enough plant-based proteins or B12 to meet their nutritional needs.

100 See the movie, *The Game Changers,* to learn about plant-based athletes.

101 See this essay by Peter Singer: https://www.theatlantic.com/ideas/archive/2023/05/vegetarian-vegan-eating-meat-consumption-animal-welfare/674150/.

102 Cultivated meat is sometimes referred to as cultured, clean, or lab-grown meat. Paul Shapiro has written a fascinating and solutionary book, *Clean Meat,* about this promising technology.

103 See "Lab-grown Meat Would 'Cut Emissions and Save Energy,'" University of Oxford, June 21, 2011, https://www.ox.ac.uk/news/2011-06-21-lab-grown-meat-would-cut-emissions-and-save-energy.

104 Visit the Good Food Institute gfi.org/ for more information about the growth of plant-based and cultivated meat and microbial protein.

105 Delicious cultured non-dairy cheeses are now available in many groceries.

106 Nondairy yogurts have become common, including oat-based, cashew-based, soy-based, and coconut-based.

107 To truly be solutionary, we also need to ensure that those producing these technologies are not exploitative in their own ways, provide afford-able proteins that are accessible to everyone, and follow environmen-tally sustainable practices throughout the production and distribution process.

108 See Donella H. Meadows et al., *The Limits to Growth: A Report for the Club of Rome's Project on the Predicament of Mankind* (New York: Universe Books, 1972), archive.org/details/limitstogrowthr00mead/page/n9/mode/2up.

Read a 50-year update here: *The Limits to Growth + 50*, Club of Rome, https://www.cluboffrome.org/ltg50/.

109 While Anne Ehrlich's name was not on the original cover of the book, she was a co-author.

110 See Nandita Bajaj and Kirsten Stade, "Challenging Pronatalism Is Key to Advancing Reproductive Rights and a Sustainable Population," *Population and Sustainability* 7, no. 1 (2023): 43, https://www.whp-journals.co.uk/JPS/article/view/819/527.

111 More than half the population of the world is expected to be in the mid-dle class by 2030 according to Omri Wallach, "The World's Growing Middle Class (2020–2030)," Elements Visual Capitalist, February 2, 2022, elements.visualcapitalist.com/the-worlds-growing-middle-class-2020-2030/.

112 See https://www.populationbalance.org/.

113 See Jayanta Kumar Bora et al., "Revisiting the Causes of Fertility Decline in Bangladesh," *Asian Population Studies* 19:1 (2023), online, doi.org/10.1080/17441730.2022.2028253, https://www.tandfonline.com/doi/full/10.1080/17441730.2022.2028253.

114 See Patricia Dérer, "Changing Social Norms and Behaviors for the Sake of the Planet and People," Overpopulation Project, overpopulation-project.com/changing-social-norms-and-behaviors-for-the-sake-of-the-planet-and-people/amp/.

115 The challenge will be to ensure that there is money to do this with a declining population. AI, discussed throughout this chapter, may play

a role in this, along with other economic and political solutions that follow in the next sections.

116 See https://www.publicpower.org/public-power.

117 See gnhusa.org/genuine-progress-indicator/.

118 See uwaterloo.ca/canadian-index-wellbeing/.

119 See https://www.oecdbetterlifeindex.org.

120 You can read more about this solution in Hinkley's 2011 book, *Time to Change Corporations: Closing the Citizenship Gap.*

121 See doughnuteconomics.org/about-doughnut-economics.

122 This has been true of many of our technologies. For example, and as previously mentioned in Population Solutions, in the 20th century, the Green Revolution led to the development and dissemination of high-yielding crop varieties, the use of synthetic fertilizers, and the expansion of irrigation systems, which in turn increased food production and improved food security for millions of people. It also resulted in environmental degradation, ocean dead zones, pollution, a loss of genetic diversity, along with the consolidation of agribusinesses and displacement of small farmers.

123 See Knut Alicke et al., "Taking the Pulse of Shifting Supply Chains," McKinsey & Company, August 26, 2022, https://www.mckinsey.com/capabilities/operations/our-insights/taking-the-pulse-of-shifting-supply-chains.

124 See https://www.nytimes.com/2023/04/07/business/economy/ai-tech-dna-supply-chain.html?referringSource=articleShare.

125 See Megan Brenan, "61% of Americans Support Abolishing Electoral College," Gallup website, September 24, 2020, news.gallup.com/poll/320744/americans-support-abolishing-electoral-college.aspx.

126 See Danielle Allen, "Introducing Power-Sharing Liberalism: A Response to Misha Chellam and Abundance Progressives," RadicalXChange Foundation, August 15, 2022: section "More *vs.* Less Trust in Existing Institutions," https://www.radicalxchange.org/media/blog/introducing-power-sharing-liberalism/.

127 As of September 2023, NPVIC has been adopted by sixteen states and the District of Columbia. These states have 205 electoral votes, which equals 76% of the 270 votes needed to give the compact legal force. For up-to-date information about the NPVIC, see https://www.nationalpopularvote.com/.

128 See Elaine Kamarck and John Hudak, "How to Get Rid of the Electoral College," Brookings Institution, December 9, 2020, https://www.brookings.edu/blog/fixgov/2020/12/09/how-to-get-rid-of-the-electoral-college/.

129 Danielle Allen, op. cit., section "Conclusion."

130 John McCain and Mark Salter, *Worth the Fighting For* (Random House, 2002).

131 See Marc A. Feigen, "How to Reform the 2024 Presidential Primaries," *Newsweek,* April 14, 2003: para 9, https://www.newsweek.com/how-reform-2024-presidential-primaries-opinion-1794011.

132 See https://www.census.gov/newsroom/press-releases/2021/2020-presidential-election-voting-and-registration-tables-now-available.html. Far fewer people vote during years in which there are only Congressional or local elections.

133 See https://www.pewtrusts.org/en/research-and-analysis/data-visualizations/2021/why-some-americans-didnt-check-the-box-in-2020.

134 Supreme Court reforms that require a constitutional amendment would be much more difficult to enact than those that don't.

135 On November 13, 2023, the Supreme Court adopted a code of ethics. Unfortunately, there is no enforcement provision. See Annie Gersh and Nina Totenberg, "The Supreme Court Adopts First-Ever Code of Ethics," NPR website, November 13, 2023, https://www.npr.org/2023/11/13/1212708142/supreme-court-ethics-code.

136 See Daniel Epps and Ganesh Sitaraman, "How to Save the Supreme Court," *Yale Law Journal* 129 (2019), https://www.yalelawjournal.org/pdf/EppsSitaramanFeature_srycu3pa.pdf.

137 In what I consider a stunning display of hypocrisy and sexism, the male customers (or johns) are not imprisoned; only the female prostitutes are.

138 See Timothy Hughes and Doris James Wilson, "Reentry Trends in the United States," Bureau of Justice Statistics, last revised April 14, 2004, bjs.ojp.gov/content/pub/pdf/reentry.pdf.

139 The school-to-prison pipeline describes the trend in which students, particularly low-income students of color, are disproportionately targeted and punished for minor infractions like tardiness, dress code violations, and talking back to teachers. Coupled with zero-tolerance policies and over-policing in schools, these kids are more likely to be arrested for

their infractions, drop out of school, face limited job prospects, become involved in gangs, break laws, and wind up incarcerated.

140 See Wendy Sawyer and Peter Wagner, "Mass Incarceration: The Whole Pie 2023," Prison Policy Initiative, March 14, 2023, https://www.prison policy.org/reports/pie2023.html. Between 1980 and 2016, the population of the United States grew from approximately 226 million to 323 million. In other words, while the population grew ~43%, incarceration grew ~503%.

141 Ibid.

142 See E. Ann Carson et al., "Impact of COVID-19 on State and Federal Prisons, March 2020–February 2021," Bureau of Justice Statistics, August 2022, bjs.ojp.gov/library/publications/impact-covid-19-state-and-federal-prisons-march-2020-february-2021.

143 The release of so many prisoners does not appear to have increased crime rates. See Masood Farivar, "How COVID-19 Jail Releases Are Impacting US Crime Rate," VOA, July 27, 2020, https://www.voanews.com/a/covid-19-pandemic_how-covid-19-jail-releases-are-impacting-us-crime-rate/6193500.html.

144 We can add to this the education and retraining of those working in prisons, so that communities where prisons are a primary employer are not adversely affected by shifts away from incarceration and can maintain healthy local economies through alternative employment opportunities.

145 See information on the successful LEAD program in Seattle. "Law Enforcement Assisted Diversion (LEAD)," King County, kingcounty.gov/depts/community-human-services/mental-health-substance-abuse/diversion-reentry-services/lead.aspx.

146 See Maria Cramer, "What Happened When a Brooklyn Neighborhood Policed Itself for Five Days," *The New York Times,* June 4, 2023, https://www.nytimes.com/2023/06/04/nyregion/brooklyn-brownsville-no-police.html?referringSource=articleShare.

147 See "Criminal Justice Fact Sheet," NAACP, naacp.org/resources/criminal-justice-fact-sheet.

148 See "A Tale of Two Countries: Racially Targeted Arrests in the Era of Marijuana Reform," ACLU, https://www.aclu.org/report/tale-two-countries-racially-targeted-arrests-era-marijuana-reform.

149 See https://www.justiceinnovationlab.org/.

150 Among the most famous are "learned helplessness" studies that shocked dogs and prevented them from escaping the shocks, and "maternal deprivation" experiments that isolated and abused baby monkeys.

See "Cruel Experiments on Infant Monkeys Still Happen All the Time—That Needs to Stop," *Scientific American,* online, June 2015, https://www.scientificamerican.com/article/cruel-experiments-on-infant-monkeys-still-happen-all-the-time-that-needs-to-stop/.

151 See Meredith Wadman, "FDA No Longer Needs to Require Animal Tests Before Human Drug Trials," *Science,* January 10, 2023, https://www.science.org/content/article/fda-no-longer-needs-require-animal-tests-human-drug-trials.

152 See Veronica Salib, "The FDA Modernization Act 2.0 Allows Animal Trials Alternatives," *PharmaNewsIntelligence,* pharmanewsintel.com/news/the-fda-modernization-act-2.0-allows-animal-trials-alternatives.

153 See Melissa Heikkilä, "DeepMind Has Predicted the Structure of Almost Every Protein Known to Science," *MIT Technology Review,* https://www.technologyreview.com/2022/07/28/1056510/deepmind-predicted-the-structure-of-almost-every-protein-known-to-science/.

See Talib Visram, "DeepMind's Latest AI Tool Could Help Create Lifesaving Cures," Fast Company, July 29, 2022, https://www.fastcompany.com/90774517/deepmind-alphafold-predicts-the-structures-of-almost-every-known-protein.

154 See "New Approach Methods Work Plan," US Environmental Protection Agency, December 2021, https://www.epa.gov/system/files/documents/2021-11/nams-work-plan_11_15_21_508-tagged.pdf.

155 Some of these solutions are ones we at the Institute for Humane Education are working to achieve.

156 See Salman Khan, "How AI Could Save (Not Destroy) Education," April 2023, TED2023 video, https://www.ted.com/talks/sal_khan_how_ai_could_save_not_destroy_education.

157 I shared some of these critical content areas in my book *The World Becomes What We Teach: Educating a Generation of Solutionaries.* Essential content might include an overview of the history of our planet, of humankind, and of the students' own nation, including the history of the original people on that land; the history of conflict and peacemaking; logic and epistemology; statistics and probability; ecology, biology,

nutrition, and psychology; climate science and climate change; media, disinformation, and conspiracy theories; and sustainable and ethical living in a globalized world.

158 You can find some of these resources here: humaneeducation.org/teach-the-solutionary-framework/.

159 The Institute for Humane Education provides free resources along with an online Solutionary Micro-credential Program, workshops, and coaching to help teachers gain the knowledge and skills they need.

160 See https://www.weareteachers.com/teacher-shortage-statistics/.

161 The percentage that property taxes contribute to school funding varies state by state.

162 See Elin Kelsey, Quotes, Quotable Quote, Goodreads, https://www.goodreads.com/quotes/10826663-hope-is-a-verb-with-its-sleeves-rolled-up-david.

Appendix 1:
The Solutionary Framework and
Solutionary Scale

Y OU HAVE SEEN this graphic illustrating the Solutionary Framework and Solutionary Scale in chapter 5, but for ease of use, I've included them here as well.

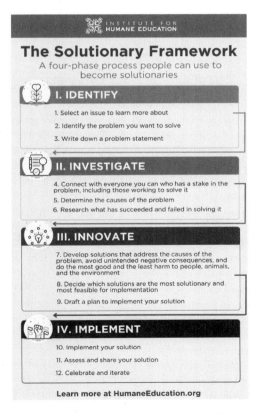

Appendix 1.1: CREDIT: INSTITUTE FOR HUMANE EDUCATION

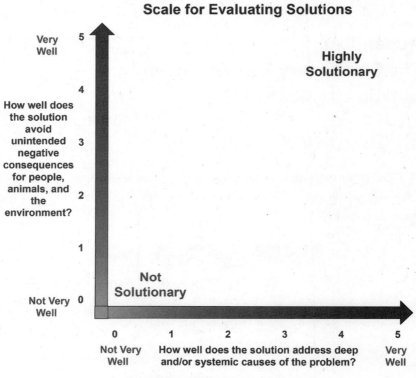

Appendix 1.2: Solutionary Scale.

CREDIT: INSTITUTE FOR HUMANE EDUCATION, BY KACEY DEWING

Appendix 2:
The Five Key Questions

YOU HAVE ALREADY considered the following questions as you've explored the solutionary process in this book, but not all together. Asking and seeking to answer these questions as a unit may prove useful. If you can find the place where the answers meet, you will likely find yourself on a powerful, meaningful, and solutionary path.

1. What issues and problems most concern you?
2. What are you good at?
3. What do you love to do?
4. What is your sphere of influence?
5. With whom can you collaborate?

Appendix 3:
The MOGO Questionnaire

E NDEAVORING TO DO THE MOST GOOD and least harm for people, animals, and the environment through our personal choices is part of being a solutionary. As chapter 2 sought to convey, our personal decisions matter because:

- Individual choices collectively lead to new systems.
- We are always modeling our message, and to the degree that each of us lives with integrity and seeks to model a message that reflects our values, we are more credible, persuasive, and influential as solutionaries.
- Living aligned with our values builds greater self-respect and inner peace.

This questionnaire gives you the opportunity to introspect and better align your choices with your values. Be gentle with yourself as you go through this questionnaire. Remember that you live embedded in systems that make it impossible to live in full alignment with your values. Recognize that psychological and biological forces are likely to periodically steer you off course. At the same time, do not let yourself off the hook: these systems and forces shouldn't be used as an excuse not to try to do the most good and the least harm to the degree that you can. I hope that you will find that striving for that sweet spot between cutting yourself slack and holding yourself to a high standard is a worthwhile effort.

1. What qualities (values) are most important to you?
    - How do you model these qualities?

- Where do you fall short in modeling them?
- What steps are you willing and able to take to model these qualities more deeply?

2. What choices do you currently make to maximize equity and justice and minimize the exploitation and/or oppression of people both in your community and nation as well as in other countries that produce and supply the products you use and foods you eat?

   - What new or different choices would you like to make to deepen your commitment to maximizing equity and justice?
   - What steps are you able to take to make this change?

3. What food, product, entertainment, and pet- and wildlife-related choices do you make to minimize the abuse toward and suffering of nonhuman animals?

   - What new or different choices would you like to make to reduce the harm you cause animals?
   - What steps are you able to take to make this change?

4. What choices do you make to live in an ecologically sustainable way?

   - What new or different choices would you like to make to live in a more ecologically sustainable way?
   - What steps are you able to take to make this change?

5. What percentage of your income do you currently donate to nonprofit organizations working to build a more equitable, humane, and sustainable future as well as to humanitarian causes to relieve suffering?

   - As you reflect on your financial needs and resources, what percentage would you like to donate to solutionary nonprofits and humanitarian organizations?
   - What steps are you able to take to make this change?

6. How much time per month do you volunteer and/or engage in advocacy, democracy, and/or solutionary work?

    • As you reflect on your capacities, how much time would you like to spend and in what ways?
    • What steps are you able to take to make this change?

7. How do you care for your physical, emotional, intellectual, and spiritual health so that you have the energy, equanimity, knowledge, and ability to be the best solutionary you can be?

    • Does anything need to change in order to take care of yourself adequately without being overly focused on yourself?
    • What steps are you able to take to make this change?

8. How will you hold yourself accountable to what you've written above?

Appendix 4:
Chart of Problems, Impacts, and
Local Manifestations

Below is a list of Problems, Impacts, and Local Manifestations that includes the issues in the chart in chapter 5 along with many other problems. While this list is relatively long, it is by no means comprehensive.

PROBLEM	IMPACTS	LOCAL MANIFESTATIONS
Climate change	• The majority of people and nations are impacted, and, to greater and lesser degrees, are perpetuating the problem. • Impacts myriad species and poses an existential threat to people and animals living on low-lying islands and in coastal regions, as well as those without the means to move or adjust to climate impacts. • Is causing increased fires, droughts, floods, heat, storms, coral bleaching, desertification, extinctions, and is creating climate refugees.	• City/regional/personal energy not from renewable sources. • Lack of convenient public transportation options and /or biking paths in my community. • Carbon-intensive foods served in local school, workplace, church/synagogue/mosque, hospital, etc.
Poverty	• Poverty leads to a host of problems, including overall human suffering,	• Poverty, homelessness, and hunger in my community.

PROBLEM	IMPACTS	LOCAL MANIFESTATIONS
Poverty	homelessness, malnutrition, lack of access to clean water, ill health, lack of access to healthcare, reduced lifespan, etc. • Poverty also leads to societal dysfunction. • Those living in poverty may have no choice but to poach wildlife or destroy habitat for fuel and resources.	• Lack of access to quality affordable healthcare in my community. • Lack of access to good jobs and affordable higher education/technical education in my community.
Modern-day animal agriculture (factory farming)	• Factory farming practices are responsible for animal cruelty, pollution, soil erosion, ocean dead zones, antibiotic resistance, and health problems. • Factory farming is one of the biggest contributors to climate change. • Slaughterhouse work is among the most dangerous jobs with workers routinely suffering debilitating injuries.	• Factory farmed products served in local school, workplace, church/ synagogue/ mosque, hospital, etc. • Lack of education in my community about the impacts of factory farming so that people can make informed dietary choices. • Few laws to protect farmed animals in my state.
Human population growth	• Leads to increasing use of finite resources. • Results in more people striving for high carbon-intensive lifestyles that are not sustainable. • Leads to increased habitat destruction, crowding, sprawl, factory farming, and monoculture agriculture systems. • Coupled with climate change, leads to increased potential for refugee crises.	• Lack of family planning education in my community. • Lack of solutionary-focused discussions to limit unwanted pregnancies. • Zoning issues in my community that lead to sprawl, traffic, conflicts with wildlife, and a reduction in natural places.

PROBLEM	IMPACTS	LOCAL MANIFESTATIONS
Slavery and trafficking	▪ Modern-day slavery of adults and children includes trafficking for both labor and sex, forced labor in a range of industries, enslaved soldiers, permanent debt bondage, and forced marriage.	▪ Lack of awareness that slavery may be occurring in my community. ▪ Lack of local resources for trafficked people to escape slavery in my community. ▪ Lack of local services and education for those who've escaped slavery in my community.
Isms (racism, sexism, classism, ableism, etc.)	▪ These isms have become embedded in societal structures and systems (to greater and lesser degrees depending upon the society and the specific ism). While efforts to address these isms have been pursued for decades and sometimes centuries, and progress has been and continues to be made, they persist. ▪ Additionally, isms do not operate in isolation and reflect interconnected systems of oppression that can magnify the harms inflicted on groups with multiple marginalized identities. ▪ (Speciesism, not included in this chart, is an ism that affects animals.)	▪ Lack of education in my school/workplace/ church/synagogue/ mosque about how to address and solve one (or more) of these structural problems where it occurs in my community. ▪ Polarization around whether to even discuss these problems in my community and in my local schools. ▪ Lack of legislation/policies to address local or state forms of structurally embedded isms.
Prejudice (anti-Black bigotry, xenophobia, homophobia/ transphobia,	▪ Prejudice refers to personal bias (as opposed to systemic structures that support societal isms). While progress has been made to reduce prejudices,	▪ Prejudice within my community (e.g., in schools, law enforcement, jails and prisons, etc.).

PROBLEM	IMPACTS	LOCAL MANIFESTATIONS
Islamophobia, antisemitism, prejudice against any group)	they still persist, and some are on the rise. • Prejudice harms those who are its victims psychologically, sometimes physically, and by limiting opportunities. It also limits the good that could be achieved by those who experience prejudice. • Prejudice harms societies in general and contributes to many of the other problems in this chart.	• Depression, rage, and despair among victims of prejudice in my community. • Lack of education and bridge-building to reduce prejudice in my community or in my local schools.
Violence (war, genocide, domestic violence, child abuse, suicide, mass shootings, etc.)	• Violence is not a new problem, and many forms of violence have declined. However, modern forms of warfare and ever more deadly and accessible weapons, coupled with a rise in depression and suicidality, make violent impulses (whether outwardly or inwardly directed) often more lethal.	• Lack of educational initiatives in my community to address and end violence locally. • Lack of conflict resolution programs to diminish violence in local schools and/or community. • Ease of getting weapons in my state without ensuring mental health and background checks.
Emerging technological risks (artificial intelligence, virtual & augmented reality, genetic engineering, surveillance)	• While modern technologies offer profound opportunities and benefits to individuals and society, they carry with them risks, some of which are quite dangerous. These include: malicious use, algorithmic bias, misuse of AI-powered autonomous weapons, unintended negative consequences of genetic engineering, the necessity for international regulations that may be difficult to secure, systems	• Lack of education about how to protect against technological dangers. • Lack of knowledge about the technologies themselves and their potential risks (e.g., not taught in schools). • Unfounded conspiracy theories about emerging technologies spreading in my community that eclipse an understanding of and focus on real risks.

PROBLEM	IMPACTS	LOCAL MANIFESTATIONS
	failures, loss of freedom, and the emergence of AGI, to name some.	
Inequity	• Inequities have been growing, rather than declining in recent decades across the globe. While more people are escaping extreme poverty, growing inequities carry threats, including conflict and deepening stratification within societies.	• Property tax policies in my state perpetuate inequities in school funding. • Zoning laws limit the ability of lower-income people to move into neighborhoods with better school districts. • Increased exposure to environmental hazards in poorer neighborhoods in my community.
Animal cruelty (not only in food production, but also trapping, hunting, poaching, fishing, animal experimentation, trafficking, poisoning, rodeos, circuses, horse and dog racing, sea parks, fur, leather, down, wool)	• While most people are opposed to animal cruelty, it persists not only in food production but also in the clothing, entertainment, research and testing, and wildlife management industries.	• Roadside zoo, sea park, animal racing (dog or horse) or other animal entertainment in my community. • Rodeo or circus coming to town. • Cruel wildlife control programs in my state or community.
Habitat destruction	• Rainforests, boreal forests, and temperate forests are being clear-cut and/or burned intentionally or through wildfires. • Coral reefs are dying. • Wild lands are being destroyed for mining. • Sensitive wetlands are being damaged.	• Clear-cutting is legal in my state/province. • New housing and/or commercial developments are threatening wild lands in my region. • A pig farm operation is polluting the waterways in my region.

PROBLEM	IMPACTS	LOCAL MANIFESTATIONS
	• Development is encroaching into natural areas. • Desertification is extending.	
Media disinformation and misinformation	• Without unbiased media sources on which people can depend for news and information, we can easily become siloed and believe things that aren't true. • Media disinformation perpetuates conspiracy thinking, anti-democratic and authoritarian movements, polarization/partisanship, and the diminishment of a well-informed citizenry capable of effectively participating in democracy and solving problems.	• Lack of media literacy and critical thinking education in my local schools. • Lack of media literacy and critical thinking education in my community. • Lack of legislation and policies to prevent disinformation in my state.
Political dysfunction (e.g., corruption, gerrymandering, money in politics, lack of free and fair elections, disenfranchisement)	• Many so-called democracies around the world are in name only, without free and fair elections and led by dictators and oligarchs. • In the United States, money in politics, corporate lobbying, redistricting/gerrymandering, voter disenfranchisement, distrust of the election process, falsehoods about voting legitimacy, etc. have resulted in a political system that is not working effectively and does not represent the majority of US citizens.	• Gerrymandering is happening locally and impacting fair elections. • Politicians in my state are working to disenfranchise voters and make voting harder. • Clean election laws, ranked choice voting, and other efforts to create a healthier democracy are missing in my state.

PROBLEM	IMPACTS	LOCAL MANIFESTATIONS
Pollution (air, soil, water)	• Pollution includes particulates, endocrine disruptors, climate change gases, manure, fertilizers, pesticides, smoke from fires, litter, microplastics, PFAS (forever chemicals), and more.	• Corruption in my county or state is enabling companies to pollute with impunity. • Superfund site in my community. • PFAS are being found in water supplies in my state.
Lack of solutionary-focused humane education	• Solutionary-focused humane education has the potential to transform all other systems by preparing students to be engaged, skilled, and knowledgeable solutionaries. Given all the problems listed here, the lack of solutionary-focused humane education in schools is itself a significant problem.	• Solutionary-focused humane education is not being offered in my local schools or district. • Local teachers lack training and knowledge to educate their students to be solutionaries. • Government officials and business leaders aren't trained to be solutionaries in my community.

Acknowledgments

A s I mentioned in the conclusion, the solutionary path has brought remarkable people into my life, and I have had the privilege to work with a phenomenal team at the Institute for Humane Education (IHE). While there are too many members of the IHE community to name individually, I am deeply grateful to our staff, faculty, board members, advisors, donors, alumni, teachers, and students for helping to make the ideas in this book take hold across the world. The fruits of IHE's efforts ultimately reside with this ever-growing, dedicated group of generous, wise, solutionary-minded people.

Three members of our team, Mary Pat Champeau, Steve Cochrane, and Julie Meltzer, read an early draft of this book and helped me to improve it significantly. One of our former faculty members, Melissa Feldman, also read this early draft with stunning attention to detail and recommending hugely important suggestions and organizational changes, almost all of which I enthusiastically incorporated. This book is so much better because of these dear friends and colleagues.

I also shared the book with people who had expertise in various issues, systems, and fields in order to hear perspectives from those with greater knowledge and more experiences than I have, especially regarding chapter 6, Solutions. A huge thank you (in reverse alphabetical order) to Howard Yaruss, Paul Shapiro, Andrew Revkin, Dana McPhall, Dave McKay, holly Kretschmar, Rudy Karsan, Tracey Katof, Steve Gross, Jared Fishman, Tami Drake, Nandita Bajaj, Mark Anderson, and Doug Alexander for offering your thoughts and perspectives. Marc Bekoff, thank you for all you have done to support my work and for your efforts on behalf of this book. To my friends the Peggys—Peggy Palmer and

Peggy Sugerman—and to Shawn Sweeney, thank you for your ideas and dedication to get this book into as many hands as possible.

I did not develop the solutionary process by myself. It was built through a collaborative effort among many people who previously worked for and/or currently work at the Institute for Humane Education. Thank you Barbara Fiore and Marsha Rakestraw, along with instructional designers Leigh Alley and David Rosen, for your work building the Solutionary Program Online Course, which was a precursor to IHE's *Solutionary Guidebook,* Solutionary Framework, and Solutionary Microcredential Program, and to Julie Meltzer, Betsy Farrell-Messenger, Mary Pat Champeau, Kris Tucker, and Steve Cochrane for continually suggesting refinements to our framework and process.

Thank you Andra Yeghoian, Doron Markus, Julia Fliss, Elizabeth Crawford, and Mitch Bickman, not only for being among my educational heroes as well as tireless solutionary educators but also for joining our IHE team to do the iceberg analysis of our current educational system, which led to much of the section on Phase II in chapter 5.

When you're an author, it's ideal to have an editor that truly supports your book's vision. It's even better when your publisher's entire mission is fully aligned with it. It's an honor and joy to work with New Society Publishers (NSP), a rare publishing company dedicated to producing solutions-oriented books for a better world as a carbon-neutral, certified B Corporation that prints on 100% post-consumer recycled paper. I'm so grateful to the entire NSP team, with special thanks to my editor Rob West and to Diane McIntosh, who designed such a beautiful cover.

To Jen Shepard and Larrance Fingerhut, thank you for teaching me improv comedy, which has provided a foundation for much of my solutionary approach, as well as for two decades of hilarity. To my fellow Bettys: the lessons and laughter are always with me.

Thank you to my CrossFit community for keeping me both physically and mentally fit. Working out in a community of people with divergent perspectives who are forever cheering each other on has made me both physically stronger and a better thinker, communicator, and a less judgmental person. Enormous gratitude to Nick Birdsall, the founder of our CrossFit affiliate and my dear friend, who built this supportive community and still believes that one day I will be able to do a strict ring muscle up. I hope he's right.

To Jane Goodall, thank you for being my hero, inspiration, and role model for more than half a century and for your tireless work to build a healthy and humane world for all. It's one of the greatest honors of my life that you wrote the Foreword to this book. "Together we can! Together we will! Together we must!"

My mother, Peggy Weil, died on March 11, 2023, shortly before I signed my contract with New Society Publishers that included a quickly approaching deadline for the completion of the manuscript. It was both a challenge and a blessing to have that deadline: a challenge because losing my mother was obviously very difficult, and a blessing because the looming deadline meant I was continuously distracted during the months following her death. My mom was a huge supporter of my work, and I felt her blessing to work with gusto even during a time of mourning.

I couldn't have finished this book by the deadline had it not been for my brother, Stanley Weil III, who oversaw the myriad tasks that follow the death of one's last living parent. Stanley, I'm so grateful for your willingness to handle those seemingly endless details so that I could focus on completing this book and for your support and belief in the importance of my work.

I cannot express gratitude for my family of origin without mentioning my beloved father, Stanley Weil Jr., who died in 1985. His was the most steadfast and unconditional love of my life, and I am fortunate beyond measure to have been showered with that love for nearly 24 years. While I've lived far longer without my dad than with him, he will always remain the most foundational role model for me for equanimity, warmth, and love. I hope some of what he modeled comes through in this book.

My husband, Edwin Barkdoll, and my son, Forest Barkdoll-Weil, are my everything. They were also the first readers of this book. Edwin is the best life partner I could ever hope for, along with being the best critical thinker I know, which meant he provided incredibly helpful feedback. Forest is the best son I could ever hope for, and he also has a keen eye for recognizing potentially polarizing writing and understanding people with perspectives so different from mine—also really helpful in a book that attempts to be an antidote to polarization.

The abundance of love, support, and humor not only from my beloved family but also from my wonderful friends (you know who you are!) is the foundation from which I am able to do what I can to make a difference. Thank you from the bottom of my heart.

About the Institute for Humane Education

T HE INSTITUTE FOR HUMANE EDUCATION (IHE) offers resources, online courses, workshops, and coaching for both educators and changemakers across the globe who are looking to build a more equitable, sustainable, and humane future for all people, animals, and the environment. IHE also offers the only online graduate programs in solutionary-focused humane education through an affiliation with Antioch University.

At IHE, we believe that a better world is possible. You can find out more and join our solutionary community at HumaneEducation.org.

Index

S

Sanders, Senator Bernie, on
  change, 17
Shatner, William, 67
Sikora, Rae, on "us vs. them," 14
Singer, Peter, 68
Single Perspective Instinct, 63
Sitaraman, Ganesh, 149
Size Instinct, 63
slavery, persistence of, 71–72
Smith, Alisa, 14
social change
  creating, 18
  negative outcomes of, 18–19
  world, social changes in, xx,
    xxi–xxii, xxiii
socialism, 130, 131, 132
social issues, newsworthiness of, xix
social systems
  changing, 56–57
  education strategy for changing,
    65
  impacts of, 56
  interplay of, 56
solutionaries
  applying the solutionary
    approach, xxiv
  being, xxii, 164
solutionariness
  assessing, 21–22
  developing, **21**
  emerging, **21**
  food waste program anecdote, 22
  most solutionary, **21**
  solutionary, **21**

solutionary
  defined, xi, 19
  ethical considerations involved,
    19
solutionary activities, creating
  change, 18
solutionary approach
  applying, xxiv, xxv
  not being taught, **92**, **94**, 95,
    97–101, **103**
  transformative power of, 66
Solutionary Framework, 65, **77**,
  183
solutionary lens
  changeability of, 17
  description, 13
solutionary mindset
  description, 13
  features of, 10
  goals of, 10
  skills involved in, 9
solutionary practice, maintaining
  personal balance, 74–75
solutionary process
  benefits of, 65–66
  outcomes of, 65–66
  self-assessment of skills, 69
  stages of, **77**
Solutionary Rubric, 21
Solutionary Scale, **117**, **184**
solutionary thinking, elements of,
  49
solutionary way
  achievements possible through,
    xv

About the Author

CREDIT: FOREST BARKDOLL-WEIL

ZOE WEIL is the co-founder and president of the Institute for Humane Education (IHE). She is the author of seven other books, including Amazon #1 best seller in the Philosophy and Social Aspects of Education, *The World Becomes What We Teach: Educating a Generation of Solutionaries;* Nautilus Silver Medal winner, *Most Good, Least Harm;* and *Above All, Be Kind: Raising a Humane Child in Challenging Times.* She has also written books for young people, including Moonbeam Gold Medal winner, *Claude and Medea: The Hellburn Dogs,* about 12-year-old activists inspired by their teacher to become solutionaries. Her blog, *Becoming a Solutionary,* can be found at PsychologyToday.com.

In 2010, Zoe gave her first TEDx talk, "The World Becomes What You Teach," which became among the 50 top-rated TEDx talks within a year. Since then she has given five other TEDx talks: "Solutionaries," "Educating for Freedom," "How to Be a Solutionary," "Extending Our Circle of Compassion," and "How Will You Answer This Question?"

Zoe is a recipient of the NCSS Spirit of America award that honors people who follow their conscience and act against current thinking in order to stand up for equity, freedom, and the American spirit of justice. She was named one of *Maine Magazine's* 50 independent leaders transforming their communities and the state and was honored with the Women in Environmental Leadership award at Unity College. Her portrait was painted by Robert Shetterly for the *Americans Who Tell The Truth* portrait series.

Zoe received a master's in Theological Studies from Harvard Divinity School; a master's and bachelor's in English Literature from the University of Pennsylvania; and was awarded an honorary doctorate from Valparaiso University. Zoe is certified in psychosynthesis counseling, a form of psychotherapy which relies upon the intrinsic power of each person's imagination to promote growth, creativity, health, and transformation.

ABOUT NEW SOCIETY PUBLISHERS

 New Society Publishers is an activist, solutions-oriented publisher focused on publishing books to build a more just and sustainable future. Our books offer tips, tools, and insights from leading experts in a wide range of areas.

We're proud to hold to the highest environmental and social standards of any publisher in North America. When you buy New Society books, you are part of the solution!

- This book is printed on **100% post-consumer recycled paper,** processed chlorine-free, with low-VOC vegetable-based inks (since 2002).
- Our corporate structure is an innovative employee shareholder agreement, so we're one-third employee-owned (since 2015).
- We've created a Statement of Ethics (2021). The intent of this Statement is to act as a framework to guide our actions and facilitate feedback for continuous improvement of our work.
- We're carbon-neutral (since 2006).
- We're certified as a B Corporation (since 2016).
- We're Signatories to the UN's Sustainable Development Goals (SDG) Publishers Compact (2020–2030, the Decade of Action).

At New Society Publishers, we care deeply about *what* we publish—but also about *how* we do business.

To download our full catalog, sign up for our quarterly newsletter, and learn more about New Society Publishers, please visit newsociety.com.

 ENVIRONMENTAL BENEFITS STATEMENT

New Society Publishers saved the following resources by printing the pages of this book on chlorine free paper made with 100% post-consumer waste.

TREES	WATER	ENERGY	SOLID WASTE	GREENHOUSE GASES
40	3,200	17	140	17,500
FULLY GROWN	GALLONS	MILLION BTUs	POUNDS	POUNDS

 Environmental impact estimates were made using the Environmental Paper Network Paper Calculator 4.0. For more information visit www.papercalculator.org

 Certified B Corporation

 new society PUBLISHERS www.newsociety.com

 FSC MIX Paper | Supporting responsible forestry www.fsc.org FSC® C016245

 SDG PUBLISHERS COMPACT

Forges a path away from polarization toward ethical problem solving and a more humane, equitable, and healthy society

Filled with both extensive examples of the problems being addressed, along with potential solutions that can be implemented. Read this book. Become a solutionary.

– SHARIFF ABDULLAH, author, *Creating a World that Works for All*

It's not enough to inspire people. We've got to equip people. That means providing tools to build skills and the motivation to use those skills. Which is exactly what this book does. Practicing the solutionary way will benefit everybody.

– IRSHAD MANJI, founder, Moral Courage College and bestselling author, *Don't Label Me*

FROM TACKLING INJUSTICE to protecting the environment to ending animal cruelty to improving the strength of our communities, deep divisions in our society often prevent us from working collaboratively to solve the problems we face.

Based on Zoe Weil's decades of work as a humane educator, *The Solutionary Way* provides clear, achievable methods to bridge divides, address the causes of seemingly intractable challenges, and create positive change. Grounded in evidence-based optimism and illustrated with dozens of real-world examples, this book provides:

- A guide to the primary components of a solutionary mindset—critical, systems, strategic, and creative thinking
- A comprehensive articulation of the solutionary framework (Identify, Investigate, Innovate, and Implement)
- A compelling argument for the MOGO principle—to do the most good and least harm for people, animals, and the environment
- An overview of emerging solutions to a variety of systemic problems
- The personal benefits associated with becoming a solutionary, from a greater sense of purpose to deeper compassion and reduced feelings of apathy and isolation.

This exciting and empowering book will appeal to a broad audience, including changemaker activists, advocates for social justice, environmental sustainability, and animal protection, business and political leaders, and anyone who yearns to contribute to a healthy, equitable and humane world.

A path toward a more ethical, meaningful life and a process toward a future where everyone, human and nonhuman, can thrive.

– MOBY, musician and activist

ZOE WEIL is the cofounder and president of the Institute for Humane Education where she created the first graduate programs preparing the leaders of the solutionary-focused humane education movement that links human rights, environmental sustainability, and animal protection. An acclaimed speaker, she is the author of eight books, including *The World Becomes What We Teach* and *Most Good, Least Harm*.

new society
PUBLISHERS

www.newsociety.com

ISBN 978-0-86571-998-9

9 780865 719989

5 2

US $22.99 / CAN $